Bicycle Vacation Guide

everything you need
to plan your
bicycle vacation

Minnesota *and* Wisconsin

Doug Shidell *and*
Vicky Vogels

LITTLE
TRANSPORT
P R E S S

Minneapolis, Minnesota

Copyright Page

Photos by Doug Shidell

Cover design by Jaana-Maria Bykonich

Interior production and design by Mori Studio

Trail information Doug Shidell

Vacation information Vicky Vogels

Maps Doug Shidell

09 08 07 06 05 04 03   10 9 8 7 6 5 4 3 2 1

Little Transport Press
P.O. Box 8123
Minneapolis, MN 55408

ISBN 0-9746625-0-X

Disclaimer: No road can be guaranteed safe. No trail is without hazards. Road and trail conditions can change without notice, and traffic conditions can change unexpectedly. The maps and descriptions are intended to aid in the selection of routes, but do not guarantee safety while riding. Use your best judgement. Ride at your own risk.

Printed in the United States.

Dedication

To the memory of Greg Marr, founder of Silent Sports Magazine; wordsmith, photographer, bicyclist, cross-country skier, friend

Acknowledgements

Special thanks to Helen Dickson, Matt and Jenn Evenson, Mike Robinson, Maggie Foote, Jan Boyum, Angela Anderson, Noreen Farrell and Lois Jorgenson Russell for making special efforts to provide information on their respective trails. Thanks to Les Phillips for making the phone calls and follow up research to guarantee the accuracy of the tourist and travel information in Bicycle Vacation Guide. Thanks also to the selfless souls in tourist booths and Chambers of Commerce throughout the region who answered our questions, mailed brochures and verified the accuracy of the information we included in Bicycle Vacation Guide. This book would not be possible without the help of these wonderful folks.

Preface

New bicycle trails don't just happen. They are the result of strong citizen support, a well organized campaign and money. We at Little Transport Press are pleased to introduce you to the non-profit group most responsible for growing and protecting hundreds of miles of state trails in Minnesota. The Parks & Trails Council of Minnesota, in coordination with local advocacy groups, has played an essential role in creating the Gateway Trail, the Cannon Valley Trail, the Paul Bunyan Trail and many more trails in Minnesota.

Since 1954, the Parks & Trails Council has been in the business of saving special places across Minnesota. In the early days, with a small membership, the group was responsible for creating Afton, Fort Snelling and Grand Portage State Parks. In more recent years, they have added almost a mile of spectacular rocky shoreline to Split Rock Lighthouse State Park and helped fund the extension of the Root River Trail in southeastern Minnesota. During the decade from 1990 to 2000, the Parks & Trails Council purchased land valued at several million dollars throughout Minnesota for eventual use as parkland and trail corridors.

The Parks & Trails Council has made this third edition of Bicycle Vacation Guide possible, and essential. Because of their efforts and those of local trail advocacy groups, Minnesota has one of the highest number of trail miles in the country and more miles are being added each year. We don't mind. Researching new trails and updating existing trails is a joy for both of us.

We joined the Parks & Trails Council, and donated hundreds of our map sets for them to use as incentives for others to join, because we see their impact each time we update our guide. Today the Council feels the urgent need to grow to bring strength to its message at the State Capitol and to keep up with the growing number of important projects that it is asked to support. We urge you to join us in supporting the Parks & Trails Council of Minnesota. To learn more, visit their website at www.parksandtrails.org or call 651-726-2457. With your help, the Parks & Trails Council of Minnesota will be able to preserve more trails and parkland for our generation and that of many generations to come.

Sincerely,

Doug Shidell and Vicky Vogels
Little Transport Press

Table of Contents

Happy trails . . .

Doug and Vicky

Gitchi-Gami State Trail Northern Minnesota

Vital Information:

Trail Distance: 8 miles

Trail Surface: asphalt

Access Points: Gooseberry Falls, Split Rock Lighthouse State Park, Beaver Bay, Many points along Hwy 61

Fees and Passes: None

Trail Website:
www.GitchiGamiTrail.com

ABOUT THE TRAIL

This trail offers some of the best bicycling views available of the North Shore of Lake Superior. It is being built piecemeal as part of overall reconstruction of Hwy 61.

The longest section, 8.4 miles, currently runs from Split Rock Lighthouse to Beaver Bay. Shorter segments have been finished near Gooseberry Falls, Tofte and Garnd Marais. Check the website for expected completion dates for new sections.

TRAIL HIGHLIGHTS

The trail segment from Split Rock Lighthouse State Park to Beaver Bay is the longest section. The trail dips into the park on a long descent, then climbs back to the Highway right of way. Excellent views of Lake Superior from the high bluffs between the park and Beaver Bay.

The 1.2 mile section near Gooseberry Falls climbs to the top of the road cut just east of the park. Great views. Start mid-trail or at the east end because the trail ends abruptly near the west end, with no motor vehicle access.

ABOUT THE ROADS

See Road Highlights for information about Scenic Drive. Highway 61 north of Two Harbors has high traffic, including trucks. It is not recommended as a bicycle route.

ROAD ROUTE HIGHLIGHTS

Scenic Drive, between Duluth and Two Harbors has low traffic, wide shoulders, great views of Lake Superior and frequent restaurants and shops for lunch breaks.

HOW TO GET THERE

From Duluth, take North Shore Drive (Highway 61). Scenic Drive begins near the east side of Duluth where the highway splits. Split Rock Lighthouse State Park is approximately 50 miles east of Duluth on Highway 61.

Gitchi-Gami State Trail   Northern Minnesota

Split Rock River to Beaver Bay 8.4 miles

Gooseberry Falls 1.2 miles

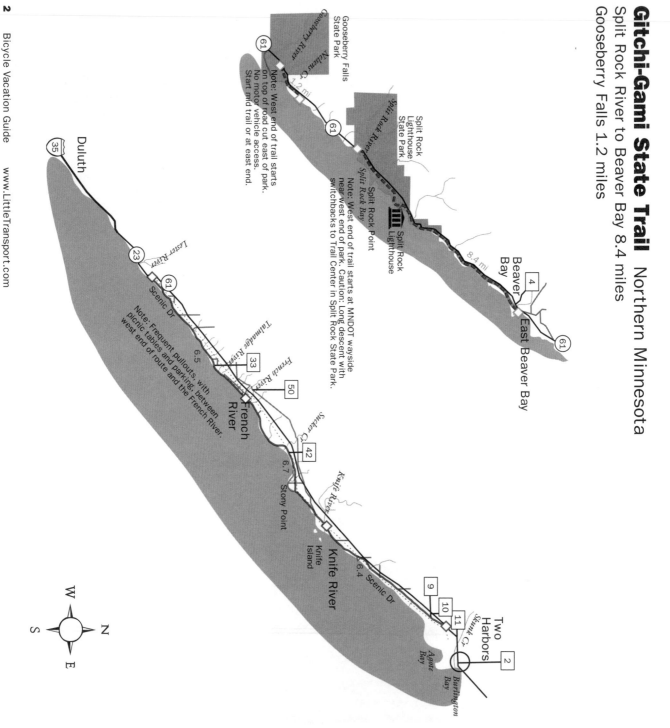

Gooseberry River

Gooseberry Falls
State Park

Note: West end of trail starts
on top of road cut east of park.
No motor vehicle access.
Start mid trail or at east end.

1.2 mi

Nelsens Cr

Split Rock River

Split Rock
State Park

Split Rock
Lighthouse
State Park

Split Rock Bay

Split Rock Point
Split Rock River

Note: West end of trail starts at MNDOT wayside
near west end of park. Caution: Long descent with
switchbacks to Trail Center in Split Rock State Park.

Split Rock
Lighthouse

8.4 mi

Beaver
Bay

East Beaver Bay

Duluth

Lester River

Scenic Dr

Palmade River

Note: Frequent pullouts, with
picnic tables and parking, between
west end of route and the French River.

6.5

French River

French River

Sucker Cr

6.7

Stony Point

Knife River

Knife River

Knife
Island

Scenic Dr

6.4

Two
Harbors

Skunk Cr

Agate
Bay

Burlington
Bay

N
W   E
S

TOURIST INFORMATION

Gitchi-Gami Trail Association
Email info@GitchiGamiTrail.com
Web www.GitchiGamiTrail.com

Lutsen/Tofte Tourism
Toll Free (888) 616-6784
Phone (218) 663-7804
Web www.61north.com

North Shore Visitor
Web www.northshorevisitor.com

Silver Bay Information Center
Phone (218) 226-3143

LODGING

Motels/Resorts

Beaver Bay
Cove Point Lodge
Hwy 61
Toll Free (800) 598-3221
Phone (218) 226-3221
Web www.covepointlodge.com

Schroeder
Lamb's Resort Cabins &
P.O. Box 415
Phone (218) 663-7292
Fax (218) 663-7057
Web www.boreal.org/lambsresort

Superior Ridge Resort-Motel
8091 W. Hwy 61
Toll Free (800) 782-1776
Phone (218) 663-7189
Email supridge@boreal.org
Web www.superiorridge.com

Temperance Traders Cabins
PO Box 58
Phone (218) 663-0111
Email info@northshorecabins.com
Web www.northshorecabins.com

Silver Bay
Lax Lake Resort & Campground
5736 Lax Lake Road
Phone (218) 353-7424
Email info@surfandturfadv.com

Tettegouche State Park
5702 Highway 61
Toll Free (888) 646-6367
Phone (218) 226-6365
Fax (218) 226-6366
Web www.stayatmnparks.com

Tofte
Americinn
P.O. Box 2249
Toll Free (800) 634-3444
Phone (218) 663-7899
Fax (218) 663-7387
Email lsameric@boreal.org
Web www.AmericInnTofte.com

Bluefin Bay on Lake Superior
P.O. Box 2125
Toll Free (800) 258-3346
Phone (218) 663-7296
Email emailus@bluefinbay.com
Web www.bluefinbay.com

Chateau LeVeaux
Box 115
Toll Free (800) 445-5773
Phone (218) 663-7223
Web www.chateauleveaux.com

Cobblestone Cabins
6660 W. Hwy 61
Phone (218) 663-7957

Sugar Beach Resort
PO Box 2236
Phone (218) 663-7595
Email bwcalandco.l.l.p.
Web www.toftesugarbeach.com

Two Harbors
Castle Haven Cabins
3067 E. Castle Danger Road
Phone (218) 834-4303

Erickson's Gooseberry Cabins
3044 E. Castle Danger Road
Phone (218) 834-3873
Email karotime@mr.net
Web webpages.onvoy.com/karotime/

Gooseberry Falls Trailside Suites
3317 Hwy 61
Toll Free (800) 715-1110

Gooseberry Park Motel/Cabins
2778 Hwy 61
Toll Free (800) 950-0283
Phone (218) 834-3751
Web www.gooseberryparkcabins.com

Grand Superior Lodge
2826 Hwy 61
Toll Free (800) 627-9565
Phone (218) 834-3796
Email info@grandsuperior.com
Web www.grandsuperior.com

LODGING cont'd

Bed and Breakfast

Beaver Bay
Northland Trails Guest House
Hwy 61
Box 521
Phone (218) 226-4199
Web www.northlandtrails.com

Two Harbors
J. Gregers Country Inn
3320 Hwy 61
Toll Free (888) 226-4614
Email jgregers@harbornet.net
Web www.jgregersinn.com
NorthernRail Traincar Suites
1730 Hwy 3
Phone (218) 834-6084
Web www.northernrail.net

Camping

Beaver Bay
Split Rock Lighthouse State Park
3755 Split Rock Lighthouse Rd
Toll Free (888) 646-6367
Phone (218) 226-6377
Web www.stayatmnparks.com

Schroeder
Lamb's Resort Cabins & Campground
P.O. Box 415
Phone (218) 663-7292
Fax (218) 663-7057
Web www.boreal.org/lambsresort
Temperance River State Park
7620 W Hwy 61
Toll Free (888) 646-6367
Phone (218) 663-7476
Web www.stayatmnparks.com

Silver Bay
Lax Lake Resort & Campground
5736 Lax Lake Road
Phone (218) 353-7424
Email info@surfandturfadv.com
Northern Exposure Campground
5346 Hwy 61 E.
Phone (218) 226-3324
Email nec@lakesuperiorcamping.com
Web www.lakesuperiorcamping.com
Tettegouche State Park
5702 Highway 61
Toll Free (888) 646-6367
Phone (218) 226-6365
Fax (218) 226-6366
Web www.stayatmnparks.com

Two Harbors
Gooseberry State Park
3206 Hwy 61
Toll Free (866) 857-2757
Phone (218) 834-3855
Fax (218) 834-3787
Web www.stayatmnparks.com

GROCERIES

Beaver Bay
Holiday Station Store
(218) 226-3227

Silver Bay
Mike's One Stop
(218) 226-4694
Silver Bay Amoco Food Shop
(218) 226-3333
Zup's Grocery & Deli
(218) 226-4161

Tofte
Holiday Station Store
(218) 663-7882
North Shore Market & Bottle
(218) 663-7288

Northern Minnesota Gitchi-Gami State Trail

BIKE RENTAL

Lutsen
Lutsen Mountain Ski Hill
Phone (218) 663-7281
Email ski@lutsen.com
Web www.lutsen.com

Tofte
Bluefin Bay Resort
Toll Free (800) 258-3346
Phone (218) 663-7860
Email www.bluefinbay.com
Web www.bluefinbay.com

Sawtooth Outfitters
Phone (218) 663-7643
Email info@sawtoothoutfitters.com
Web www.sawtoothoutfitters.com

FESTIVALS AND EVENTS

Schroeder
September
John Schroeder Day
Festivities commemorating Schroeder history.
Downtown near Cross River Bridge, food vendors, craftsmen, artists, kids games, musical entertainment and spaghetti dinner.
World famous minnow races daily plus raffle drawings. Call for dates.
Phone (218) 663-7706

Tofte
July
Independence Day Celebration
Tofte Trek, parade, food, music and fireworks at dusk, Tofte Town Park, Fourth of July
Toll Free (888) 616-6784
Phone (218) 663-7804
Web www.61north.com

East Beaver Bay
Lake Superior Excursions Aboard the Grandpa Woo
Board the 40 passenger Grandpa Woo at the public launch in East Beaver Bay or Agate Bay in Two Harbors and tour Superior's coastline. Highlights include the craggy shoreline, river mouths, Silver Cliff, Encampment Island, Split Rock Lighthouse and Palisade Head.
Phone (218) 226-4100
Email gwoo@gulftel.com
Web www.grandpawoo.com

Schroeder
Captain Kelly Charters
Scenic fishing trips aboard the High Tide
Phone (218) 370-8050
Email schliep@lakenet.com
Web www.northshorevisitor.com/captainkelly

Sugarloaf Interpretive Center
Visit interpretive displays about geology, ecology, and culture of the North Shore. Specially arranged hikes, programs & rental of the Interpretive Center are available. Open May - September on Saturdays & Sundays.
Phone (218) 663-7679

Temperance River State Park
The Temperance River drops 162 feet in a half mile in a series of cascades, the last of which occurs about 100 feet from its mouth at Lake Superior. Large potholes and cauldrons in the gorge. The park has a fishing stream and 6 miles of foot trails.
Phone (218) 663-7476

ALTERNATE ACTIVITIES

Naturalist Programs
US Forest Service Resort Naturalist
Program on everything from bears to moose and voyageurs to wildflowers. A wide variety of family-oriented nature activities. The programs are hosted by many of the resorts & hotels. All programs are free & available to everyone regardless of where you may be staying on the shore. There are morning & evening programs daily, Tuesday through Saturday. For times, locations, & topics, see posted schedules at participating locations.
Phone (218) 663-8060

Beaver Bay
Kayaking-Lake Superior Water Trail
The State of Minnesota has set up a water trail for sea kayakers along the shores of Lake Superior. It will eventually extend the entire way around Lake Superior.
Email berndt.abes@juno.com
Web http://www.lswta.org

Silver Bay

Palisade Head

Incredible views of Lake Superior, Shovel Point and 200-foot cliffs. Off Hwy 61 about 4 miles NE of Silver Bay, watch for signs. Follow the gravel road to the top. Open seasonally.

Silver Bay's Bayside Park

Boat landing, picnic tables, fire pits, and a beach. Pick agates on the beach, hike a short trail to a scenic lookout. Located on the shore of Lake Superior off Hwy 61 just east of Beaver Bay/west of Silver Bay.

Tettegouche State Park

Hike to rocky, wind-swept Shovel Point or back into one of the four, quiet inland lakes. Don't miss the beautiful High Falls on the Baptism River, the highest waterfall inside Minnesota's borders. 16 miles of hiking trails. Tettegouche Camp is on the National Register of Historic Places; cabins of the old hunting camp are now rented as walk, bike, or ski-in lodging.
Phone (218) 226-6365

Tofte

Carlton Peak

The highest peak on the MN North Shore—927 feet about lake level. Scenic hiking trails—3.4 miles round-trip to the peak or 5.2 miles round-trip to the overlook. From Hwy 61 in Tofte, go north on the Sawbill Trail (Co. Rd. 2) for 2 miles to the parking area on the east/right Walk across the Sawbill Trail and follow the snowmobile trail.
Phone (218) 834-2700
Email suphike@mr.net
Web www.shta.org

Lake Superior Sport Fishing

Relaxing and scenic fishing trips with Tofte Charters
Toll Free (800) 258-3346
Phone (218) 663-9932
Email Darren@toftecharters.com
Web www.toftecharters.com

North Shore Commercial Fishing Museum

Exhibits take you across the cultural landscape of North Shore commercial fishermen and their families. Gallery, lectures, presentations and ongoing programs
Phone (218) 663-7804
Email info@commercialfishingmuseum.org
Web www.commercialfishingmuseum.org

Two Harbors

Gooseberry Falls State Park

On the Lake Superior shoreline with 5 waterfalls, historic log and stone buildings, wayside rest, picnic grounds. Visitor center has exhibits, nature store, trail center and naturalist pro-

grams. 18 miles of hiking trails and 12 miles of mountain bike trails. River and Lake Superior fishing.
Phone (218) 834-3855
Fax (218) 834-3787
Web www.stayatmnparks.com

Split Rock Lighthouse

Split Rock Lighthouse was built on top of a 130 foot cliff in 1910. Tour the lighthouse, fog signal building and keeper's home. Exhibits and film in history center. Adjacent to Split Rock Lighthouse State Park
Phone (218) 226-6377
Web splitrock.lighthouse@dnr.state.mn.us

Superior Hiking Trail

Begins just north of Two Harbors, MN, and ends just before the Canadian border. The 235-mile trail connects seven state parks and features waterfalls, rivers, lakes, and diverse forests. Foot travel only.
Phone (218) 834-2700
Email suphike@mr.net
Web www.shta.org

Mesabi Trail

Vital Information:

Trail Distance: 46 miles

Trail Surface: asphalt

Access Points: Grand Rapids, Coleraine, Bovey, Taconite, Hibbing, Chisolm, Buhl, Kinney, Mt. Iron, Virginia, Gilbert, Eveleth

Fees and Passes: $3 per day, $6 per week, $12 annual.

Trail Website: www.mesabitrail.com

ABOUT THE TRAIL

From Grand Rapids to Gilbert, the trail dips, rolls and twists its way from mining town to open pit. It skirts the edge of active mines and 300 foot deep pit lakes. It wanders down the back streets of small towns, hooks up with abandoned roads and runs next to old rail lines with aspens sprouting between the rail ties. The Iron Range is full of history and everything from museums and mine views to the long hills of mine tailings reflects its active industrial past.

The Mesabi Trail never wanders far from that history. The trail is being developed in sections. The 40 mile stretch from Grand Rapids to Kinney is finished in all but one 8 mile segment. The next largest section, from Mt. Iron to Eveleth, covers 15 miles. This is an ideal trail for anyone who likes a few hills and a lot of history.

TRAIL HIGHLIGHTS

The 15 mile stretch from Mt Iron to Eveleth is the most charming, with the prettiest stretch between Gilbert and Virginia. In Virginia, follow Veteran's Drive through Olcott Park. Allow some time in the park to explore the greenhouse and enjoy the flower gardens. The Hibbing section is the richest in Iron Range history. The Greyhound Bus Origin Museum and Hull Rust Mahoning Mine View are both within blocks of the Hibbing Trailhead. The Trailhead in Grand Rapids starts from the north end of the fairgrounds, then skirts the edge of a pit lake where a huge wedge of mine tailings juts into it like the prow of a ship in harbor. Later

it crosses the Prairie River and works its way to the sleepy town of Taconite. If you have time, take the spur trail to Gunn Park, a donation from the Blandin Foundation.

ABOUT THE ROADS

Paved roads are limited in the area and the through routes usually carry a lot of traffic. It's possible to take short out and back trips from some of the towns but if you want to make loops on low traffic roads, expect to ride long sections of gravel.

ROAD HIGHLIGHTS

None

HOW TO GET THERE

Highway 169 goes straight north from the Twin Cities to Grand Rapids, then connects the Range cities along the trail. Turn south on Highways 53/135, near Virginia, and follow Highway 135 to the Gilbert trailhead. Highway 53 from Duluth runs due north to Eveleth and Virginia near the eastern end of the trail. Travel distance from the Twin Cities to the Range cities is approximately 200 miles, depending on your destination.

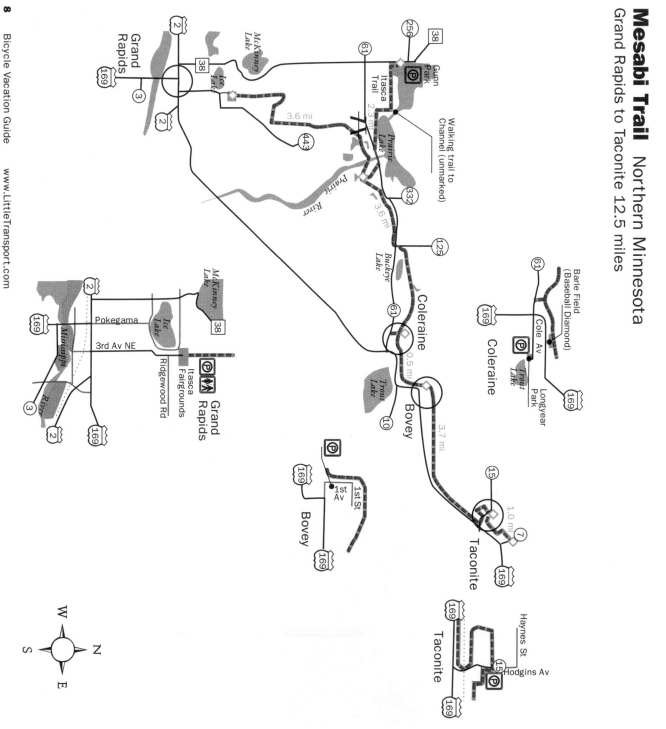

Northern Minnesota **Mesabi Trail**
Nashwauk to Eveleth 40.4 miles

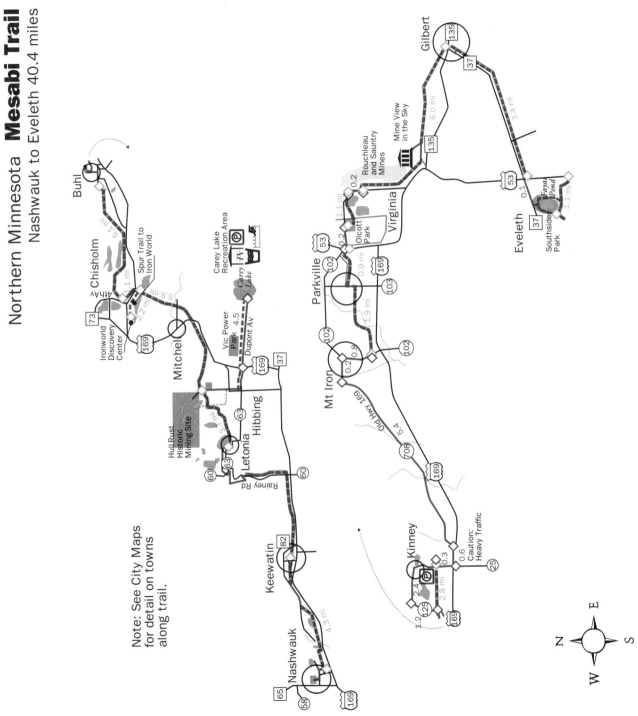

Note: See City Maps for detail on towns along trail.

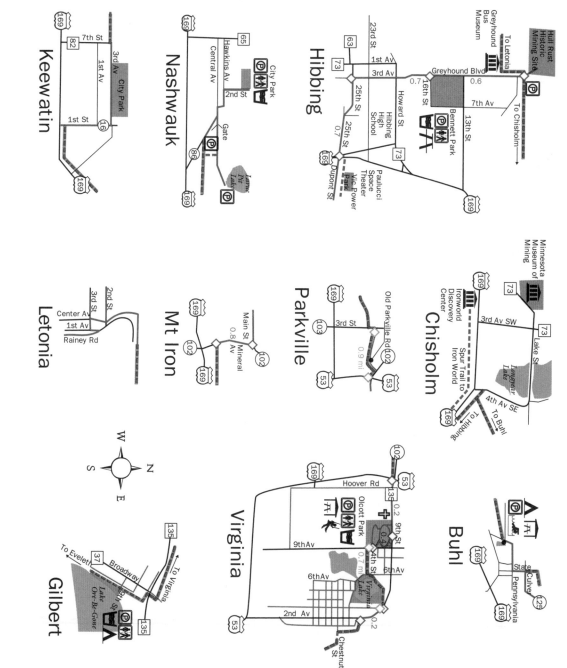

Northern Minnesota **Mesabi Trail**

Chisholm Area Chamber of Commerce
Toll Free (800) 422-0806
Phone (218) 254-7930
Email chisholm@cpinterent.com
Web www.chisholmmnchamber.com

City of Biwabik
Phone (218) 865-4183
Fax (218) 865-4580
Email info@cityOfBiwabik.com
Web www.cityofbiwabik.com

City of Gilbert City Hall
Phone (218) 748-2232
Fax (218) 748-2234
Email clerk@gilbertmn.org
Web www.gilbertmn.org

City of Mountain Iron
Phone (218) 748-7570
Email cityadmn@mtniron.com
Web www.mtniron.com

Grand Rapids Area Convention & Visitors Bureau
Toll Free (800) 355-9740
Phone (218) 326-6619
Email answers@visitgrandrapids.com
Web www.visitgrandrapids.com

Hibbing Area Chamber of Commerce
Phone (218) 262-3895
Fax (218) 262-3897
Email hibbcofc@hibbing.org
Web www.hibbing.org

Iron Trail Convention & Visitors Bureau
Toll Free (800) 777-8497
Phone (218) 749-8161
Email info@irontrail.org
Web www.irontrail.org

Trail Central
Toll Free (877) 637-2241
Phone (218) 742-9543
Email info@mesabitrail.com

Virginia/Mt Iron Area Chamber of Commerce
Phone (218) 741-2717
Fax (218) 749-4913
Email vchamber@virginiamn.com
Web www.virginiamn.com

Motels/Resorts

Chisholm
Chisholm Suites
Hwy 169
Toll Free (877) 255-3156
Phone (218) 254-2000

Eveleth
Super 8 Motel
Hwy 53
PO Box 555
Toll Free (800) 800-8000
Phone (218) 744-1661

Grand Rapids
AmericInn
1812 S. Pokegama Ave
PO Box 435
Toll Free (888) 950-8999
Phone (218) 326-8999
Fax (218) 326-9190

Country Inn
2601 S. Hwy 169
Toll Free (800) 456-4000
Phone (218) 327-4960

Forest Lake Motel
W. Hwy 2
Toll Free (800) 622-3590
Phone (218) 326-6609

Itascan Motel
610 S. Pokegama Ave
Toll Free (800) 842-7733
Phone (218) 326-3489
Email info@itascan.com
Web www.itascan.com

Rainbow Inn
1300 E Hwy 169
Toll Free (888) 248-8050
Phone (218) 326-9655

Sawmill Inn
2301 South Hwy 169
Toll Free (800) 804-8006
Phone (218) 326-8501

Super 8 Motel
1702 S. Pokegama Avenue
Toll Free (800) 800-8000
Phone (218) 327-1108

Hibbing
Hibbing Park Hotel and Suites
Hwy 169 & Howard St
Toll Free (800) 262-3481
Phone (218) 262-3481
Fax (218) 262-1906
Email hibbpark@rangebroadband.net
Web www.hibbingparkhotel.com

Super 8 Motel
1411 40th St
Toll Free (800) 800-8000
Phone (218) 263-8982
Fax (218) 263-8982

Virginia
AmericInn Lodge & Suites
Hwy 53N
Toll Free (888) 741-7839
Phone (218) 741-7839
Fax (218) 741-9050

LODGING cont'd

Lakeshore Motor Inn Downtown
404 N. 6th Ave
Toll Free (800) 569-8131
Phone (218) 741-3360

Park Inn
502 Chestnut St
Toll Free (800) 777-4699
Phone (218) 749-1000
Fax (218) 749-6934
Email genmgr@parkinnvirginia.com
Web www.parkinnvirginia.com

Ski View Motel
903 N. 17th St
Toll Free (800) 255-7106
Phone (218) 741-8918

Bed and Breakfast

Hibbing
Adams House
201 E. 23rd St
Toll Free (888) 891-9742
Phone (218) 263-9742
Web www.adamshousebedandbreakfast.com

Camping

Biwabik
Vermilion Trail Park Campground
P.O. Box 529
Biwabik, MN 55708

Phone (218) 865-4183
Web www.cityofbiwabik.com

Buhl
Buhl Campground
PO Box 704
Phone (218) 258-3226
Fax (218) 258-3796

Gilbert
Sherwood Forest Campground
P.O. Box 548
Toll Free (800) 403-1803
Phone (218) 748-2221
Email campground@gilbertmn.org

Grand Rapids
Itasca County Fairgrounds
1336 NE 3rd Ave
Phone (218) 326-6470

Prairie Lake Campground & RV Park
30730 Wabana Rd
Phone (218) 326-8486

Mountain Iron
West Two Rivers Campground &
Recreation Area
4988 Campground Road
Phone (218) 748-7570
Fax (218) 748-7573
Email parks@mtniron.com

Side Lake
Bear Lake State Forest Campground
McCarthy Beach State Park
7622 McCarthy Beach Road
Phone (218) 254-7979

GROCERIES

Gilbert
Shusterich Market
(218) 741-4326

Grand Rapids
Ogle's Foods
(218) 326-9695

Hibbing
Super One Foods
(218) 262-5275

Virginia
Festival Foods
(218) 741-3229

Natural Harvest Food Coop
(218) 741-4663

BIKE RENTAL

Biwabik
Giant's Ridge Resort
Phone (218) 865-4152

Grand Rapids
Itasca Bike Ski and Fitness
Phone (218) 326-1716

BIKE REPAIR

Biwabik
Giants Ridge Resort
Phone (218) 865-4152

Grand Rapids
Itasca Trail Sports
Phone (218) 326-1716

Virginia
Mesabi Recreation
Phone (218) 749-6719

FESTIVALS AND EVENTS

Chisholm

June
International Polka Fest
At Ironworld, non-stop polka music by
35 polka bands performing on 4
stages, daily dance contest, Polka
Hall of Fame inductions, polka mass,
ethnic food, Fourth Weekend
Toll Free (800) 372-6437
Phone (218) 254-7959
Web www.ironworld.com

Rock the Range
Hosted by Chisholm area businesses, showcases local and national talent, blues and rock, Second Weekend
Toll Free (800) 422-0806
Phone (218) 254-7930
Web www.chisholmmnchamber

August

St. Louis County Fair
Exhibits, food, entertainment, midway, at Ironworld, First Weekend
Toll Free (800) 372-6437
Phone (218) 254-7959

September

Chisholm Fire Days
Kiddie parade, softball tourney, city-wide garage sales, food vendors, street dance, Second Weekend
Toll Free (800) 422-0806
Phone (218) 254-7930
Web www.chisholmmnchamber

Gilbert
July

4th of July Celebration
Huge parade, street dance, and fire-works July 3rd, kiddie parade and games. July 4th
Phone (218) 741-9443

Grand Rapids
June

Judy Garland Festival
Mingle with the original Munchkins who appeared in the Wizard of Oz: guest celebrities, Taste of Grand Rapids, film festival, collector's exchange and seminars. Fourth Weekend

Toll Free (800) 664-5839
Phone (218) 327-9276

July

Wood Craft Festival
Forest History Center, Third Weekend
Toll Free (800) 355-9740

August

Itasca County Fair
Itasca County Fairgrounds, Third Weekend
Toll Free (800) 355-9740
Phone (218) 326-6619
Web www.visitgrandrapids.com

Tall Timber Days
Downtown at the Old Central School, logging displays and events, street fair. First full Weekend
Toll Free (800) 355-9740

Phone (218) 326-6619
Web www.visitgrandrapids.com

White Oak Rendezvous
Colorful reenactment of French Voyager rendezvous. First full Weekend
Toll Free (800) 355-9740
Phone (218) 326-6619
Web www.visitgrandrapids.com

Hibbing
Dylan Days
Celebrate the life and music of Bob Dylan.
Refer to web site for dates.
Phone (218) 262-3895
Web www.hibbing.org/dylan

Mesabi Trail Northern Minnesota

July

July

Mines and Pines Jubilee

Ten day celebration, parade, street dance, arts and crafts displays and sales, fly-in breakfast, golf tourney, radio flyer show, flea market, fireworks, ice-cream social, childrens' day events, Second Weekend

Toll Free (800) 444-2246

Phone (218) 262-3895

Mountain Iron

July

4th of July Celebration

Old-fashioned celebration, sports tourneys, polka bands, watermelon eating contest, five minute parade, First Weekend

Phone (218) 748-7570

August

Merritt Days

Commemorating the discovery of iron ore in the area, street dance, parade, pet show, live music, food vendors, Second Weekend

Phone (218) 748-7570

Virginia

June

Land of the Loon Festival

At Olcott Park and downtown, parade,

14   Bicycle Vacation Guide   www.LittleTransport.com

jugglers, food vendors, arts and crafts, music, Third Weekend

Phone (218) 749-3020

Biwabik

Giants Ridge

Over 75 miles of mountain biking trails, hiking trails, disc golf, 18 hole championship golf course.

Toll Free (800) 688-7669

Phone (218) 865-3000

Fax (218) 865-3025

Email info@giantsridge.com

Web www.giantsridge.com

Chisholm

Ironworld Discovery Center

Tours, exhibits and climb-on equipment displays, electric trolley, concerts, living history exhibits, ethnic restaurant. Accessible via spur trail from the Mesabi Trail.

Toll Free (800) 372-6437

Phone (218) 254-7959

Web www.ironworld.com

Minnesota Museum of Mining

Mining trucks, steam locomotive, 1910 Atlantic steam shovel, early diamond drills, replica underground mine and mining town, open daily end of May to mid-Sept

Toll Free (800) 422-0806

Phone (218) 254-5543

Email chisholm@cpinterent.com

Web www.chisholmnchamber.com

Eveleth

US Hockey Hall of Fame

Displays of enshrined players, exhibit and film library, shooting rink, Zamboni display, theater and gift shop, open year 'round

Toll Free (800) 443-7825

Phone (218) 744-5167

Web www.ushockeyhall.com

Veteran's Lake Park

Swimming beach, picnic area, camping

Phone (218) 744-2360

Gilbert

Iron Range Historical Society and Museum

Housed in Gilbert's old City Hall /Police Station/Jail building, includes sleds used by the Will Steger North Pole Expedition, a mining exhibit, an old time jail, and research library, open Mon–Wed & Sat May–Sept

Phone (218) 749-3150

Grand Rapids

Children's Discovery Museum

Blend of permanent and changing educational exhibits. Open: Monday–Saturday 10:00am–5:00pm, Sunday 12:00 Noon–5:00pm

Toll Free (866) 236-5437

Phone (218) 326-1900

Fax (218) 326-1934

Email office@cdmkids.org

Web www.cdmkids.org/index.html

Double K Stables
27734 Scenic Dr
Phone (218) 245-3814

Forest History Center
Open air living history center operated by the Minnesota Historical Society, with full sized 1900 logging camp, costumed interpreters. Open 7 days a week, June 1–Oct 15.
Toll Free (800) 355-9740
Phone (218) 327-4482
Fax (218) 327-4483
Email foresthistory@mnhs.org
Web http://www.mnhs.org

Judy Garland Birthplace
Restored childhood home, including Judy Garland memorabilia and the carriage from the Wizard of Oz, educational hands-on exhibits in the museum
Toll Free (866) 236-5437
Phone (218) 327-9276
Fax (218) 326-1934
Email jgarland@uslink.net
Web www.judygarlandmuseum.com

Mississippi Melody Showboat
Outdoor theater on the banks of the Mississippi, last three weekends of July
Toll Free (800) 355-9740
Phone (218) 326-6619
Email answers@visitgrandrapids.com
Web www.visitgrandrapids.com

Old Central School
Turn of the Century Schoolhouse converted into marketplace, specialty shops, restaurant, Itasca County Heritage Center
Toll Free (800) 355-9740
Phone (218) 326-6431
Email answers@visitgrandrapids.com
Web www.visitgrandrapids.com

Hibbing

Greyhound Bus Origin Museum
Vintage buses, models and artifacts from the 1900s, open Mon-Sat 9AM–5PM mid-May–Sept. Located at the Hibbing Trailhead.
Phone (218) 263-5814
Fax (425) 699-0717
Email gom@cpinternet.com
Web www.greyhoundbusmuseum.org

Hibbing High School
National Register of Historic Places, hand painted murals, cut glass chandeliers, 1800 seat auditorium and more, open Mon-Sat (summers), by appointment during school year
Phone (218) 263-3675

Hull Rust Mahoning Mine
National Historic Place. World's largest open pit mine. Mine exhibits, scenic views, walking trail, at the Hibbing Trailhead, open daily from Memorial Day to Labor Day.
Phone (218) 262-4900
Fax (218) 262-3897
Email hibbcofc@hibbing.org
Web http://www.hibbing.org

Palucci Space Theater
70mm wide-screen movies on various topics, multimedia presentations, gift shop, open year 'round, call for hours
Phone (218) 262-6720
Web www.spacetheatre.mnscu.edu

Ore

Vince Shute Wildlife Sanctuary
View wildlife black bears in a natural setting from an elevated observation deck, open 5 until dusk summer evenings, about 20 miles north of Virginia.
Phone (218) 757-0172
Email bears@rangenet.com
Web www.americanbear.org

Virginia

Heritage Museum
Maintained by the Virginia Area Historical Society. Permanent exhibits housed in historical cabins and former park superintendent's residence.
Phone (218) 741-1136
Web www.virginia-mn.com

Mineview in the Sky
Overlooks the Rouchleau Mine Group, the area's deepest mine. Accessible directly from the Trail via a steep driveway. Open daily May-Sept, 8 AM–7 PM
Phone (218) 741-2717

Olcott Park Greenhouse
Profusion of flowers and plants, some exotic, some common household plants, located in Olcott Park near the heart of Virginia, open daily June–Labor Day, weekdays rest of the year
Phone (218) 748-7509

Itasca State Park

Vital Information:

Trail Distance: 5 miles

Trail Surface: asphalt

Access Points: Many points in Itasca State Park

Fees and Passes: State Park sticker for motor vehicles

Trail Website:
www.dnr.state.mn.us/state_parks

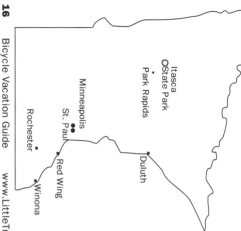

ABOUT THE TRAIL

A narrow, gently rolling trail that runs parallel to Park Drive. Frequent spurs give cyclists access to all of the high-lights of the park including scenic overlooks, a Pioneer Cemetery, camp-grounds and the headwaters of the Mississippi River.

TRAIL HIGHLIGHTS

The 0.4 mile long boardwalk north of the campground is unique and fun to ride. Check out the tombstones at the Pioneer Cemetery and take time to relax on the large shaded picnic grounds along the trail.

ABOUT THE ROADS

Bikes are discouraged from using Park Road from the visitor center to the headwaters. Traffic is heavy and the road is narrow. Use the trail instead of the road. Wilderness Drive is a beauti-ful, one way, roller coaster of a ride through deep forests and past remote lakes in the western part of the park. The road is designated a bike route by the Department of Natural Resources. Traffic is low and slow moving.

ROAD HIGHLIGHTS

Wilderness Drive is the highlight of the Park, but the lesser known Park Drive south of the Visitor Center is quite attractive and generally draws very lit-tle traffic. Make a loop by going out the south entrance of the park, then going north on Hwy 71 and Hwy 200 North until you get to the north entrance to the park. Finish the loop either on the bike path or Wilderness Drive. Hwys 71 and 200 may have heavy traffic during summer months. Both roads have good shoulders.

HOW TO GET THERE

From the Twin Cities, take Interstate 94 west to Sauk Centre. Go north on Highway 71 to Itasca State Park. The East entrance to the park is the most frequently used entrance. Travel time is about 5 hours.

Northern Minnesota **Itasca State Park**

Trail 5.8 miles
Wilderness Drive 9.6 miles

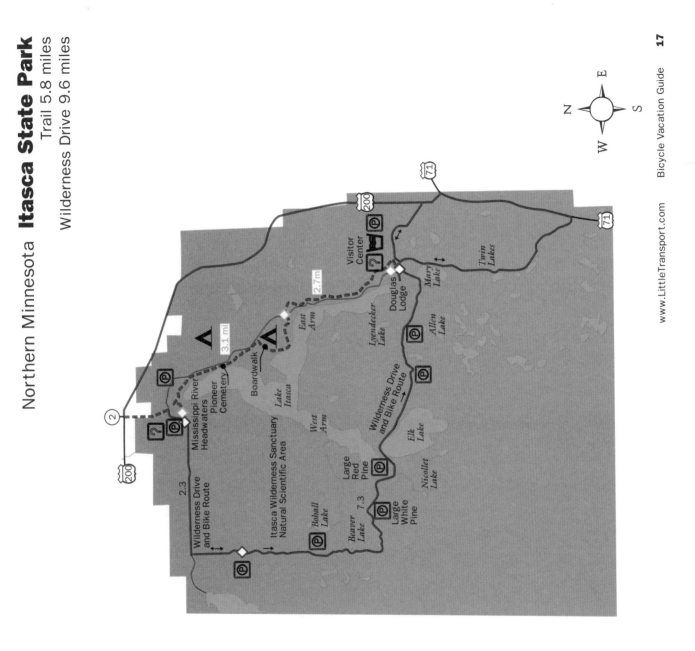

Itasca State Park
Northern Minnesota

Itasca Area Lakes
Toll Free (888) 292-7118
Phone (218) 732-8816
Email iala@wcta.net
Web www.itascaarea.com

Itasca State Park
Phone (218) 266-2100
Email itasca.park@dnr.state.mn.us
Web www.dnr.state.mn.us

LODGING

Motels/Resorts

Bert's Cabins
HC05 Box 1
Phone (218) 266-3312
Web www.bertscabins.com

Mississippi Headwaters Hostel
Itasca State Park
HC05 Box 5A
Phone (218) 266-3415
Email itascamn@aol.com
Web www.himinnesota.org/headwaters

Lake George

Lake George Pines Motel
37197 US 71
Phone (218) 266-3914

Melahn All Season Resort
Hc 70 Box 2206
Phone (218) 266-3354

Park Rapids

Itasca State Park
36750 Main Park Drive
Toll Free (800) 857-2757
Phone (218) 266-2100
Email itasca.park@dnr.state.mn.us
Web www.stayatmnparks.com

Little Norway Resort
32016 Little Mantrap Dr
Phone (218) 732-5480
Fax (218) 732-0963

Email lnorway@wcta.net
Web www.littlenorwayresort.com

Weigelwood Resort
56698 310th St
Toll Free (800) 943-3357
Phone (218) 732-4775
Email weigelwood@hotmail.com
Web www.weigelwood.20m.com

Wilderness Bay Resort & Campground
36701 Wilderness Bay Dr
Phone (218) 732-5608
Email resort@wildernessbay.com
Web www.wildernessbay.com

Bed and Breakfast

Park Rapids

Loon Song B&B
Lake Itasca
Box 27

Toll Free (888) 825-8135
Phone (218) 266-3333
Fax (218) 266-3383
Email dljohnst@djam.com
Web www.bbhost.com/loonsongbnb

Camping

Camp Itasca
4608 Williston Road
Minnetonka, MN 55345
Phone (952) 938-4097
Email campitasca@msn.com
Web www.campitasca.com

Long Lake Park & Campground
213 Main Avenue North
Bagley, MN 56621-8309
Phone (218) 657-2275
Email camp@longlakepark.com
Web www.longlakepark.com

Northern Minnesota Itasca State Park

LODGING cont'd

Park Rapids

Freedom Ridge ATV Resort
10694 State Highway 200
Toll Free (877) 266-4295
Phone (218) 266-3938
Email freedomridge@wcta.net
Web www.freedomridgeresort.com

Itasca State Park
36750 Main Park Drive
Toll Free (800) 857-2757
Phone (218) 266-2100
Email itasca.park@dnr.state.mn.us
Web www.stayatmnparks.com

Wilderness Bay Resort & Campground
36701 Wilderness Bay Dr
Phone (218) 732-5608
Email resort@wildernessbay.com
Web www.wildernessbay.com

GROCERIES

Itasca State Park
Ken's Convenience Store
(218) 266-3996

Lake George
Woodland Store
(218) 266-3468

Laporte
Lake Alice Store
(218) 266-3482

BIKE RENTAL

Itasca State Park
Itasca Sports Rental
Phone (218) 266-2150
Email info@itascasports.com
Web www.itascasports.com

FESTIVALS AND EVENTS

Itasca State Park

July

Butterfly Hike
Itasca State Park. Local butterfly enthusiast shows intro video, then leads group on 1-2 mile hike looking for butterflies. Call for date.
Phone (218) 266-2100
Web www.dnr.state.mn.us

August

Pioneer Farmer's Show
See grain threshing, lumber sawing, shingle making, and more the way it was done 'in the old days. Take a ride in a horse-drawn covered wagon or model railroad large enough to carry passengers. Check out the world's largest display of hot-air engines. Call for date.
Phone (218) 657-2233
Web http://pioneerfarmers.tripod.com

September

Ozawindib Walk
Itasca State Park. Named after an Ojibway guide and interpreter. A fundraising event, public is invited. Get a t-shirt if you walk the 1-2 mile distance. Call for date.
Phone (218) 266-2100
Web www.dnr.state.mn.us

Lake George

July

Blueberry Festival
Carnival, pie sale, pig roast, and the Blueberry Ball. Call for date.
Phone (218) 266-2915
Web www.lakegeorgemn.com

Park Rapids

September

Headwaters 100 Bike Ride
Follow a well-marked route through lakes area, Wilderness Drive in Itasca State Park and the Heartland Trail. Ride starts and ends in Park Rapids. Fourth Weekend.
Toll Free (800) 247-0054
Phone (218) 732-4111
Web www.parkrapids.com/eve

Itasca State Park Northern Minnesota

Boat Rental
Itasca State Park. Boat, motor, pontoon, paddleboat, kayak and canoe rental located across from park headquarters. Excursion boat located below Douglas Lodge on Lake Itasca.
Phone (218) 266-2100
Email itasca.park@dnr.state.mn.us
Web www.dnr.state.mn.us

Hiking
Explore over 30 miles of hiking trails, and the history of the oldest state park in MN. Maps available at the Visitor Center.
Phone (218) 266-2100
Email itasca.park@dnr.state.mn.us
Web www.dnr.state.mn.us

Lake Itasca Tours
Get a comprehensive overview of the history, wildlife, points of interest and services of Itasca State Park on a naturalist narrated boat tour to the Headwaters of the Mississippi River.
Phone (218) 732-5318
Email itasca.park@dnr.state.mn.us
Web www.dnr.state.mn.us

Mississippi Headwaters
Explore the source of the mighty Mississippi River at Itasca State Park. The Mississippi is the third longest river in the world.
Phone (218) 266-2100
Email itasca.park@dnr.state.mn.us
Web www.dnr.state.mn.us

Naturalist led programs and walks
Join naturalist led walks and programs at Itasca State Park. Get current schedule at the Visitor Center or DNR calendar on the website.
Phone (218) 266-2100
Email itasca.park@dnr.state.mn.us
Web www.dnr.state.mn.us

Swimming
Itasca State Park. Sand beach located on the North Arm of Lake Itasca.
Phone (218) 266-2100
Email itasca.park@dnr.state.mn.us
Web www.dnr.state.mn.us

Heartland Trail Northern Minnesota

Vital Information:

Trail Distance: 50 miles

Trail Surface: asphalt

Access Points: Park Rapids, Dorset, Nevis, Akeley, Walker, Cass Lake

Fees and Passes: none

Trail Website: www.dnr.state.mn.us

ABOUT THE TRAIL

From Park Rapids to Akeley, the land is quite flat with a mix of pine woodlots, farmland and lakes. The trail passes through a glacial moraine between Akeley and Walker and the surrounding land becomes hilly and pine forested. The eleven Crow Wing Lakes along Hwy 33 are examples of kettles formed when large blocks of ice from the retreating glacier were buried in dirt. Eventually the ice melted, leaving deep depressions, or kettles that filled with water. The trail follows the shore of Leech Lake for much of the way from Walker to Cass Lake.

TRAIL HIGHLIGHTS

Heartland Park in Park Rapids is a better place to start than the official trailhead on the south side of Highway 34. See city map. This is Paul Bunyan Country. The theme is overdone, but indulge in a little kitsch and sit in the hand of Paul. He's on one knee for you in the town of Akeley. Dorset is a popular starting point on the trail. This little town barely merits a wide spot in the road, but has Mexican food, Italian food, antique stores, etc.

ABOUT THE ROADS

The two routes between Park Rapids and Nevis feature medium sized rolling hills and a mosaic of lakes, woods and farmland. Watch and listen for Loons on the lakes and check out the mon-eyed homes along the eastern edge of Fish Hook Lake.

ROAD HIGHLIGHTS

Highways 12 and 6 between Akeley and Hackensack offer a connector between the Heartland and Paul Bunyan Trails. These are good roads even if you just go out and come back. Highway 12 out of Walker is paved, low traffic and has a shoulder, then turns to gravel at the Hubbard County Line. It's a good 10 mile out and back route. County Road 26 connects the Heartland Trail to the northern edge of the Paul Bunyan Trail at Hwy 34. The road has loose gravel. A trail connector is planned for the near future.

HOW TO GET THERE

From the Twin Cities, take Interstate 94 west to Sauk Centre. Go north on Highway 71 to Park Rapids. Take Highway 34 east from Park Rapids to get to access points along the trail. Park Rapids is about 5 hours from the Twin Cities. From Duluth, take Highway 2 west to Cass Lake. Start in Cass Lake or go south on Highway 371 to Walker. Take Highway 34 west from Walker for additional access points along the trail.

Heartland Trail Northern Minnesota
Park Rapids to Cass Lake 50 miles

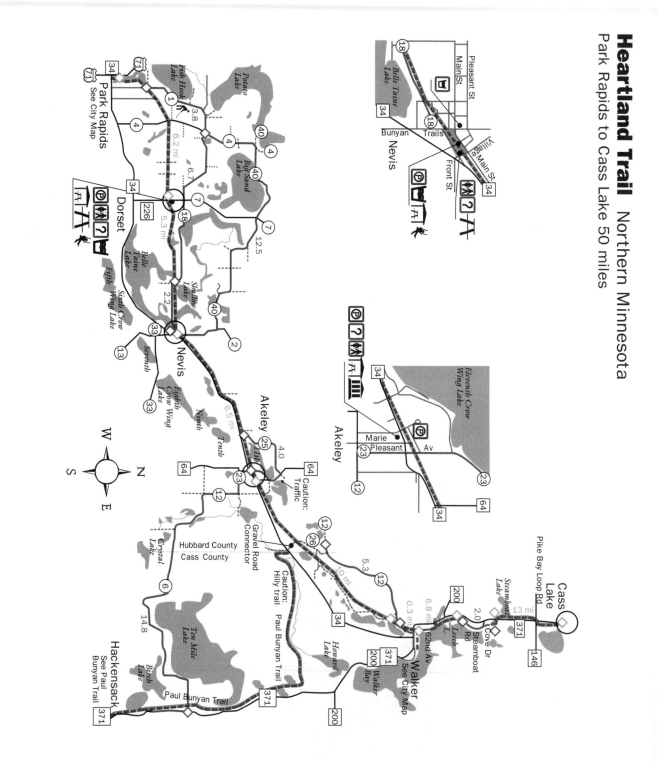

Northern Minnesota **Heartland Trail**
City Maps

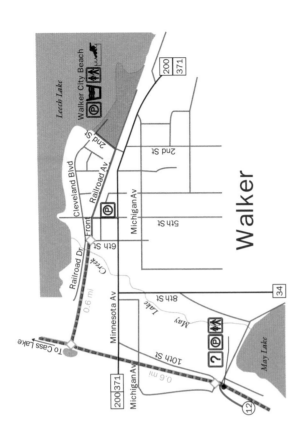

Walker

Leech Lake

Walker City Beach

2nd St

2nd St

Cleveland Blvd

Railroad Av

Michigan Av

5th St

Front St

6th St

Railroad Dr

Creek

0.6 mi

Minnesota Av

8th St

May Lake

10th St

Michigan Av

0.6 mi

To Cass Lake

May Lake

200 371

200 371

34

12

N
E
S
W

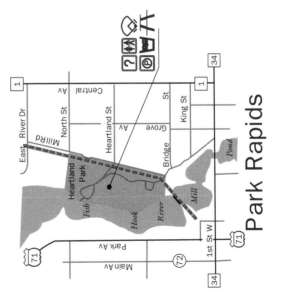

Park Rapids

East River Dr

Mill Rd

North St

Central Av

Heartland St

Grove Av

King St

St

Bridge

Heartland Park

Fish

Hook

River

Mill

Pond

Park Av

Main Av

1st St W

1
1
34
34
71
71
72

TOURIST INFORMATION

Akeley Civic & Commerce Association
Phone (218) 652-2600
Web www.akeleyminnesota.com

DNR Trails and Waterways, Nevis
Phone (218) 652-4054

Leech Lake Chamber of Commerce
Toll Free (800) 833-1118
Phone (218) 547-1313
Email info@leech-lake.com
Web www.leech-lake.com

Nevis Civic & Commerce Association
Phone (218) 652-3474
Fax (218) 652-6280
Web http://www.nevismn.com

Park Rapids Area Chamber of Commerce
Toll Free (800) 247-0054
Phone (218) 732-4111
Fax (218) 732-4112
Web www.parkrapids.com

LODGING

Motels/Resorts

Akeley

Crow Wing Crest Lodge
11th Crow Wing Lake
31159 County Road 23

Toll Free (800) 279-2754
Phone (218) 652-3111
Web www.crowwing.com

Nevis

Nevis Welcome Inn Motel & RV Park
117 Highway 34
PO Box 485
Phone (218) 652-3600

Paradise Cove Resort
21428 County 80
Toll Free (800) 765-2682
Phone (218) 732-3779
Fax (218) 732-3779
Email view@visitparadisecove.com
Web www.visitparadisecove.com

Park Rapids

Gramma's Riverview Cabins
900 N. Park Ave.
Toll Free (888) 272-1240
Phone (218) 732-0987
Email grammasbb@unitelc.com
Web http://customer.unitelc.com

Walker

City Dock Cottages
5th and Leech Lake
PO Box 544
Phone (218) 547-1662

Lakeview Inn
PO Box 1359
Toll Free (800) 252-5073
Phone (218) 547-1212
Web www.walkermn.com

Bed and Breakfast

Nevis

The Park Street Inn
106 Park St
Toll Free (800) 797-1778
Phone (218) 652-4500
Web www.parkstreetinn.com

Park Rapids

Dickson Viking Hus B&B
202 E. 4th St.
Toll Free (888) 899-7292
Phone (218) 732-8089
Fax (218) 732-2927
Email iaia@wcta.net
Web www.itascaarea.net

Gateway Guest House
203 Park Ave N
Toll Free (877) 558-8614
Phone (218) 732-1933
Web www.gatewayguesthouse.com

Heartland Trail B&B
Rt #3, Box 39
Phone (218) 732-3252
Email corbidpj@aol.com
Web www.heartlandbb.com

Camping

Itasca State Park

Itasca State Park Campground
HC05, Box 4
Toll Free (866) 857-2757
Phone (218) 266-2100
Web www.itasca.park@dnr.state.mn.us

Park Rapids

Big Pines Tent & RV Park
501 S. Central Ave.
Toll Free (800) 245-5360
Phone (218) 732-4483

LODGING cont'd

Mantrap Lake State Forest
Campground
607 W. 1st St., Hwy 34
Phone (218) 732-3309

Walker
Shores of Leech Lake Campground &
Marina
6166 Morriss Point NW
Phone (218) 547-1819
Fax (218) 547-3490
Email loomis@shoresofleechlake.com
Web www.shoresofleechlake.com

GROCERIES

Park Rapids
J & B Foods
(218) 732-3368

Walker
Bieloh's IGA
(218) 547-1624

Walker
Back Street Bike and Ski Shop
Phone (218) 547-2500
Email bikenski@paulbunyan.net
Web www.backstreetbike.com

FESTIVALS AND EVENTS

Akeley
June
Paul Bunyan Days
Fish fry, treasure hunt, pie social,
cake walk, kiddy parade and grand
parade on Sunday afternoon, arts,
crafts and food booths line the street,
Friday night teen dance, Saturday
night adult dance, Fourth Weekend
Phone (218) 652-2600
Web www.akeleyminnesota.com

BIKE RENTAL

Dorset
Heartland Trail B&B
Phone (218) 732-3252
Email corbidpj@aol.com
Web http://www.heartlandbb.com

Walker
Back Street Bike and Ski Shop
Phone (218) 547-2500
Email bikenski@paulbunyan.net
Web www.backstreetbike.com

BIKE REPAIR

Akeley
Hardware Hank
Phone (218) 652-2369

Park Rapids
Northern Cycle
Phone (218) 732-5971

Dorset

August

Taste of Dorset
Stroll down the Boardwalk to sample a variety of foods from local restaurants, Dorset boasts the reputation of having the most restaurants per capita in the USA, First Weekend
Toll Free (800) 247-0054
Phone (218) 732-4111

Nevis

August

Northwoods Triathalon
.25 mile swim begins and ends at the city beach located on Lake Belle Taine, bike 14 miles on paved roads through scenic countryside and run 5K on the Heartland Trail. Call for date.
Toll Free (218) 652-2052
Web http://www.nevis.k12.mn.us

Park Rapids

June

Hubbard County Shell Prairie Fair
Grandstand shows, demo derby, exhibitors, food vendors, midway, 4H exhibits, Fourth weekend
Toll Free (800) 247-0054
Phone (218) 732-9672

July

4th of July Celebration
Firecracker Foot Race, fireworks at city beach, First Weekend
Toll Free (800) 247-0054
Phone (218) 732-4111

Summertime Arts and Crafts Festival
Exhibitors, music, food vendors, Third Weekend
Toll Free (800) 247-0054
Phone (218) 732-4111

August

Antique Tractor Show
Threshing, tractor and horse plowing, shingle making, steam engines, square dance, parade, horse and wagon rides, Fourth Weekend
Toll Free (800) 247-0054
Phone (218) 732-5073

September

Fall Fishing Classic
$8,000 purse, First Saturday
Toll Free (800) 247-0054

Headwaters 100 Bike Ride
Loops through Itasca State Park, scenic back roads and part of the Heartland Trail. Fourth Weekend
Toll Free (800) 247-0054

Walker

July

4th of July
Parade, fireworks, food, music, children's games, volleyball, horseshoes, sumo wrestling, First Weekend
Toll Free (800) 833-1118
Phone (218) 547-1313

Moondance Jam
Moondance Fairgrounds, jam sessions, big name and regional performances, Second weekend
Toll Free (877) 666-6526
Phone (218) 547-1055

Yikes! Bikes!
18, 40 and 60 mile routes using the Heartland and MI-GI-ZI Trails. Third Saturday.
Phone (218) 547-3322
Web www.lakesareahabitat.org

August

Cajun Fest
Moondance Fairgrounds, Cajun style food, parades, dancing, music direct from Louisiana. Check website for details.
Toll Free (877) 544-4879
Web www.northernlightcasino.com

Phone (218) 732-3366

September

Annual Ethnic Fest
Downtown Walker, celebration of ethnic diversity, food vendors, craft demos, entertainment, storytelling, Second Weekend
Toll Free (800) 833-1118
Phone (218) 547-1313
Web www.leech-lake.com

Walker North Country Marathon
10K run/walk, 2 person team marathon, Third Weekend
Toll Free (800) 833-1118
Phone (218) 547-3327
Web www.leech-lake.com

ALTERNATE ACTIVITIES

Tamarac National Wildlife Refuge
43,000 acres of sanctuary and breeding ground for migrating birds and other wildlife, Visitor Center has hiking trails and picnic area
Phone (218) 847-2641
Web http://midwest.fws.gov/Tamarac

Akeley

Paul Bunyan Museum
Located on Main Street behind the statue of Paul Bunyan, the museum contains a collection of pictures and artifacts portraying early Akeley history when the state's largest sawmill was operating.
Phone (218) 652-2600
Web www.akeleyminnesota.com

WoodTick Musical Theatre
Summer musical theater featuring talent from 100 mile radius. See website for details.
Toll Free (800) 644-6892
Phone (218) 652-4200
Web www.woodticktheater.com

Cass Lake

Chippewa National Forest
Drive the Woodtick Trail, hike the Shingobee Hills or canoe the Boy River
Phone (218) 547-1044

LaPorte

Forestedge Winery
Small batch organic wines made from blueberry, chokecherry, cranberry. Plum, raspberry and rhubarb
Phone (218) 224-3535
Web www.forestedgewinery.com

Park Rapids

Itasca State Park
Visit the source of the Mississippi River, camp, bike, hike and canoe, view stands of old-growth pine over 200 years old. See Itasca Bike Trail.
Phone (218) 266-2100
Fax (218) 266-3942
Email itasca.park@dnr.state.mn.us
Web www.dnr.state.mn.us

Walker

Cass County Museum and Pioneer School House
Library, archival files, photos, newspapers, also houses Indian Art Museum, open daily 10–5, closed Sundays
Phone (218) 547-7251
Web www.leech-lake.com

Moondance Ranch & Wildlife Park
Wildlife park, trail rides, pony corral, trout pond, water slide, hot tub, hay rides, go-karts, mini golf, arcade and restaurant
Phone (218) 547-1055
Web www.moondanceranch.com

Shopping, Shopping, and more Shopping
Downtown Walker
Toll Free (800) 833-1118
Web www.leech-lake.com

Paul Bunyan Trail

Vital Information:

Trail Distance: 63 miles

Trail Surface: asphalt

Access Points: Baxter, Merrifield, Nisswa, Pequot Lakes, Jenkins, Pine River, Backus, Hackensack, Hwy 34

Fees and Passes: none

Trail Website:
www.paulbunyantrail.com

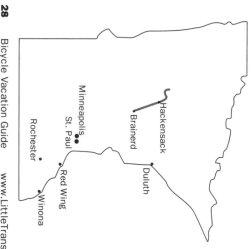

ABOUT THE TRAIL

This former Burlington Northern Rail line is ideal for biking or in-line skating. The trail more or less follows Highway 371 from Backus/Brainerd to Hackensack, then dips and rolls through the Chippewa National Forest. A half mile gravel road connects it to the Heartland Trail. Most of the small towns along the trail have parks, trailside facilities, and a lake or swimming area. Views include cattail marshes, cedar swamps, small lakes and mixed farmland/woodlot. The stretches near Highway 371 are generally wooded opposite the highway and open towards the highway.

ABOUT THE ROADS

Roads near the northern end are mostly gravel or heavily traveled. More paved, lake roads between Baxter and Nisswa, but expect traffic on weekends and holidays.

ROAD HIGHLIGHTS

Highways 17 and 1 offer a good alternate to the trail between Pequot Lakes and Pine River. See the Heartland Trail for a great connector between Hackensack on this trail and Akeley on the Heartland Trail.

TRAIL HIGHLIGHTS

The newest part of the trail is also the most unique. From Hackensack to the Chequamegon National Forest is flat, then the trail gets very hilly and winds around many sweeping turns. Inexperienced riders and skaters should use caution when entering this portion. Merrifield to Nisswa: A seven mile blend of farm fields, woodlots and wetlands, the trail has an open feel to it, yet not barren. From Backus to north of Hackensack, the trail passes through 15 remote miles of cattail marshes and cedar swamp with occasional upland woods. From the south, begin your ride at Lion's Park in Merrifield. It has excellent restrooms, sheltered picnic area and children's play area. Check out the swimming area behind the dam at the Pine River Day Use Park. Relax or swim at the city park in Backus.

HOW TO GET THERE

Brainerd is 130 miles northwest of the Twin Cities and 113 miles southwest of Duluth. Follow 210 west about 2 miles from Brainerd to Hwy 371. See city map for trail access at Baxter. All other trail towns, except Merrifield, are along Hwy 371. To start at Merrifield, take Hwy 25 north, about seven miles, from Brainerd.

Northern Minnesota **Paul Bunyan Trail**
Baxter to Pequot Lakes 21 miles

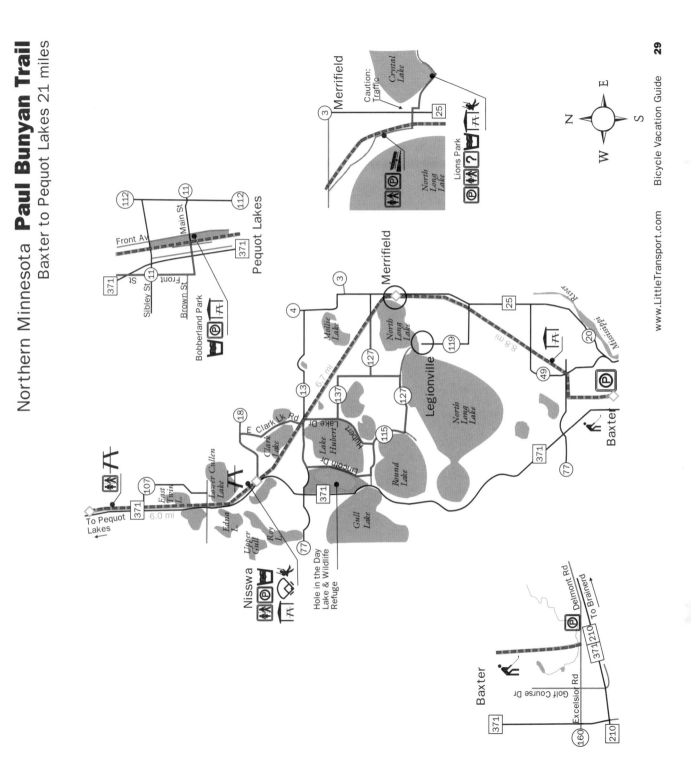

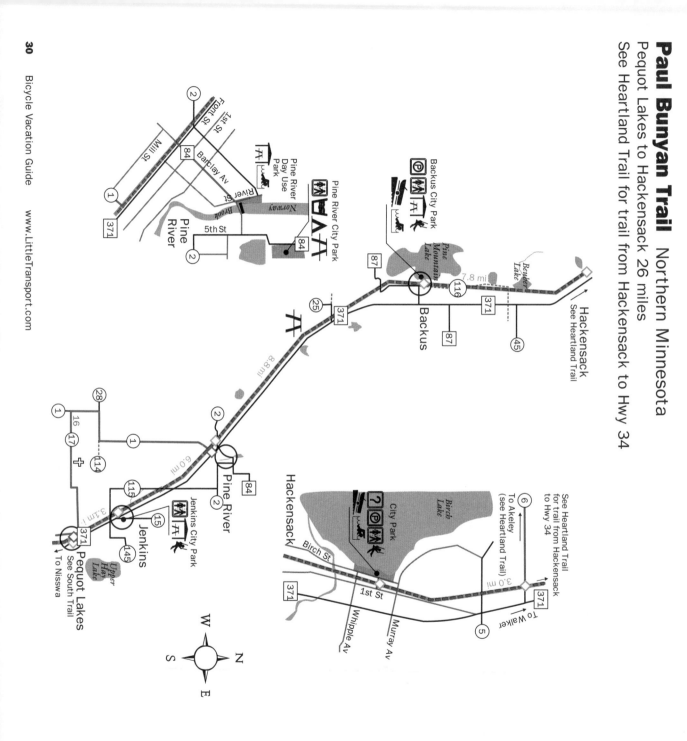

Paul Bunyan Trail Northern Minnesota
Pequot Lakes to Hackensack 26 miles
See Heartland Trail for trail from Hackensack to Hwy 34

TOURIST INFORMATION

Backus City Hall
Phone (218) 947-3221
Fax (218) 947-3221
Email clerk@uslink.net
Web www.backusmn.com

Brainerd Lakes Area Chamber of Commerce
Toll Free (800) 450-2838
Phone (218) 829-2838
Email info@explorebrainerdlakes.com
Web www.explorebrainerdlakes.com

Cass County Information Web Site
Web http://www.casscomn.com

DNR Trails and Waterways, Brainerd
Phone (218) 828-2557
Web www.dnr.state.mn.us

Hackensack Chamber of Commerce
Toll Free (800) 279-6932
Phone (218) 675-6135
Email chamber@hackensackchamber.com
Web www.hackensackchamber.com

Nisswa Chamber of Commerce
Toll Free (800) 950-9610
Phone (218) 963-2620
Fax (218) 963-1420
Email info@nisswa.com
Web www.nisswa.com

Pequot Lakes Tourist Information Bureau
Toll Free (800) 950-0291
Phone (218) 568-8911
Email info@pequotlakes.com
Web www.pequotlakes.com

Pine River Information Center
Toll Free (800) 728-6926
Phone (218) 587-4000
Web www.pinerivermn.com

LODGING

Motels/Resorts

Backus

Bayside Cabins
206 Rosalind Ave. W.
Toll Free (800) 840-3344
Phone (218) 947-3344
Fax (218) 947-4144
Email bayside@uslink.net
Web www.baysidecabins.com

Mountain View Resort
590 Wood Street North
Phone (218) 947-3233
Email mountainviewresort@tds.net
Web www.mtnviewresort.com

Hackensack

Birch Haven Resort
P.O. Box 243
Phone (218) 675-6151
Fax (218) 675-5779
Email bhresort@uslink.net
Web www.birchhavenmn.com

Happiness Resort on Ten Mile Lake
4609 Happiness Lane N.W.
Phone (218) 675-6574
Email happines@uslink.net

Hyde-A-Way Bay Resort
3489 Ford Drive N.W.
Toll Free (800) 309-5253

Phone (218) 675-6683
Fax (218) 675-6683

Shady Shores Resort
5445 Lower Ten Mile Lake Road N.W.
Phone (218) 675-6540
Email shadyshores@tds.net

Nisswa

Good Ol' Days Family Resort
P.O. Box 358
Toll Free (800) 227-4501
Phone (218) 963-2478
Email info@goodoldaysresort.com
Web www.goodoldaysresort.com

Treehouse Cottage
P.O. Box 83
Phone (218) 568-8480
Email jgweso@aol.com

Pequot Lakes

AmericInn Lodge & Suites
Hwy. 371 & City Road 16
P.O. Box 579
Toll Free (888) 568-8400
Phone (218) 568-8400
Web www.upnorthlodge.com

Bed and Breakfast

Brainerd

Whiteley Creek Homestead
12349 Whiteley Creek Trail
Toll Free (877) 985-3275
Phone (218) 829-0654
Email whiteleycrk@aol.com
Web www.whiteleycreek.com

Camping

Backus

Lindsey Lake Campground
3781 State Hwy 87 NW
Phone (218) 947-4728
Email info@lindseylake.com
Web www.lindseylake.com

Paul Bunyan Trail Northern Minnesota

LODGING cont'd

Brainerd
Crow Wing State Park Campground
3124 State Park Rd
Phone (218) 825-3075
Web www.dnr.state.mn.us

3124 State Park Rd
Phone (218) 825-3075
Rock Lake State Forest Campground

Hackensack
Quietwoods Campground & Resort
4755 Alder Lane N.W.
Phone (218) 675-6240

Pequot Lakes
Tall Timbers Campground
3823 County Road 17
Phone (218) 568-4041

Pine River
River View RV Park
3040 16th Ave. SW
Phone (218) 587-4112
Email riverviewrv@tds.net

GROCERIES

Hackensack
Mark's Market
(218) 675-6825

Nisswa
Schafer's Foods
(218) 963-2265

Pequot Lakes
Northern Food King
(218) 568-5995

Pine River
Carl's Market
(218) 587-4449

Jerry's Super Valu Amoco
(218) 587-2488

BIKE RENTAL

Backus
Bayside Cabins and Bike Rental
Toll Free (800) 840-3344
Phone (218) 947-3344

Brainerd
Easy Rider Bicycle & Sport Shop
Phone (218) 829-5516

Trailblazer Bikes
Phone (218) 829-8542

Hackensack
Mike's
Phone (218) 675-6976
Web www.mikesreel.pagehere.com

Paul Bunyan Trail Sports
Phone (218) 675-5590
Web www.brainerd.com

Merrifield
Train Bell Resort
Toll Free (800) 252-2102

Phone (218) 829-4941
Web www.trainbellresort.com

Nisswa
Trailblazer Bikes
Phone (218) 963-0699

Pequot Lakes
Bunyan Bike Shuttle and Rental
Phone (218) 568-8422
Web www.brainerd.com

Pine River
Riverview RV Park
Phone (218) 587-4112
Email riverviewrv@tds.net

BIKE REPAIR

Brainerd
Easy Riders Bicycle and Sport Shop
Phone (218) 829-5516

Trail Blazer
Phone (218) 829-8542

Hackensack
Mike's
Phone (218) 675-6976
Web www.mikesreel.pagehere.com

Paul Bunyan Trail Sports
Phone (218) 675-5590
Web www.brainerd.com/bikeshuttle

BIKE REPAIR cont'd

Nisswa
Trail Blazer
Phone (218) 963-0699

BIKE SHUTTLE

Brainerd
Easy Riders Bicycle and Sport Shop
Phone (218) 829-5516

Pequot Lakes
Bunyan Bike Shuttle and Rental
Phone (218) 568-8422
Web www.brainerd.com

FESTIVALS AND EVENTS

Backus

May

Annual Smelt Fry First Weekend
Phone (218) 947-3221

Annual Yard Sale
Sponsored by Lions Club, Memorial
Day Weekend
Phone (218) 947-3221

Old Timer's Weekend
Old time music, horseshoe tournament, ice cream bars and Sloppy Joe's
at Firehall, Memorial Day Weekend.
Phone (218) 947-3221

August

Annual Cornfest
Corn feed, parade, games, music, tal-
ent show (kids and adult divisions),
Second Saturday
Phone (218) 947-3221

Brainerd

June

Crow Wing Encampment
Fur trade era encampment with crafts
of the era, shooting demonstration,
leather and beadworking, at Crow
Wing State Park following 10 mile

canoe trip from Kiwanis Park,
Sponsored by Cross Lake Historical
Society. Call for dates
Phone (218) 825-3075

July

4th of July Celebration
Festivities spread out over several days
Toll Free (800) 450-2838
Phone (218) 829-5278

Art in the Park
Juried artists, entertainment, food,
Gregory Park, Fourth Weekend
Toll Free (800) 450-2838
Phone (218) 829-5278

August

Eastern Star Antique Show
Regional vendors, National Guard
Armory, Last Weekend
Phone (218) 829-6787

Hackensack

All Summer

Kids' Fishing Contest
At city pier from 11:00 to 1:00, every
Tuesday mid-June to mid-August
Toll Free (800) 279-6932
Phone (218) 675-6135

Lions Pancake Breakfast
Community Building, 7:30 - 11:00 am,
First Sunday of every month
Toll Free (800) 279-6932
Phone (218) 675-6135

Flea Market
Parking lot of Sacred Heart Church,
Second Wednesdays summer months
Phone (218) 675-7775

June

Sweetheart Canoe Derby
Canoe races, food vendors, craft fair,
Third Weekend
Toll Free (800) 279-6932
Phone (218) 675-6135

Sweetheart Days
Mid-week event including antique car
show, parade, horseshoe tourney, carnival, and street dance, Preceded by
performances of "Ballad of Lucette,"
a light operetta at the Community
Building, Second Weekend
Toll Free (800) 279-6932
Phone (218) 675-6135

**Volunteer Fire Dept. Fundraiser BBQ &
Dance**
Third Weekend
Toll Free (800) 279-6932
Phone (218) 675-6135

October

Northwoods Arts Festival
Regional and local artists, community
and senior center, First Weekend
Toll Free (800) 279-6932
Phone (218) 675-6135

Nisswa

All Summer

Turtle Races
Behind the Chamber of Commerce,
2:00 pm every Wednesday afternoon
Mid-June through August
Toll Free (800) 950-9610
Phone (218) 963-2620

July

Freedom Day Parade
Fourth of July celebration, stagecoach
rides, food court, parade, no fireworks
Toll Free (800) 950-9610
Phone (218) 963-2620

Garden Club Show
Hosted by Nisswa Garden Club at
Grand View Convention Center, Fourth
Weekend
Toll Free (800) 950-9610
Phone (218) 963-2620

Majestic Pines Arts Festival
Juried show, food concessions, Fourth
Weekend
Toll Free (800) 950-9610
Phone (218) 963-2620

August

Krazy Days
Community celebration, downtown,
including sales, food, weightlifting
competition.
Toll Free (800) 950-9610
Phone (218) 963-2620

Pequot Lakes

July

Bean Hole Days
150 gallons of Pequot Lakes baked
beans cooked overnight in the ground,
served between noon and 2 pm, arts
and crafts, Bobberland Wayside Trail
Park, Wednesday following the 4th
Toll Free (800) 950-0291
Phone (218) 568-8911
Web www.pequotlakes.com

July 4th Celebration
Fireworks night of 3rd, celebration
through Bean Hole Days, on 4th,
parade, baby race, liar's contest, bed
races, pie eating contest, haystack,
greased pole, foot races, food vendors.
Toll Free (800) 950-0291
Phone (218) 568-8911
Web www.pequotlakes.com

September

**Pequot Lakes Arts and Crafts Fair
And Taste of Pequot**, regional arts and
crafts, local food vendors, Trailside,

Third Weekend
Toll Free (800) 950-0291
Phone (218) 568-8911
Web www.pequotlakes.com

Pine River

All Summer

Duck Races
Decoys only, Pine River Dam, 1:00 pm
every Friday late June through mid-
August
Toll Free (800) 728-6926
Phone (218) 587-4000
Web www.pinerivermn.com

June

Summerfest
Craft and sidewalk sales, band and
gospel music, parade, golf, softball and
horseshoe tournaments, fly-in breakfast
at the airport, Legion steak fry, fire-
men's street dance, Fourth Weekend
Toll Free (800) 728-6926
Phone (218) 587-4000

FESTIVALS AND EVENTS cont'd

July

Cass County Fair
Varies, usually third weekend in July
Toll Free (800) 728-6926
Phone (218) 587-4000
Web www.pinerivermn.com

Pine River Art Show
Exhibits, sales, demonstrations, snacks, at the Pine River Elementary School
Toll Free (800) 728-6926
Phone (218) 587-4000

September

Quilting Festival
Quilt show, various exhibits, food, music, Pine River churches. Call for festival date.
Toll Free (800) 728-6926
Phone (218) 587-4000

ALTERNATE ACTIVITIES

Brainerd

Crow Wing County Historical Society
Local history, logging, railroad and mining history, located in the old county jail/sheriff's residence, call for hours
Phone (218) 829-3268
Email history@brainerd.net
Web www.rootsweb.com/~mncwcghs

Crow Wing State Park
Remains of the town of Old Crow Wing, site of the confluence of Crow Wing and Mississippi Rivers, hiking trails
Toll Free (218) 825-3077
Phone (218) 825-3075
Web www.dnr.state.mn.us

Kart Kountry at Vacation Land Park
Bumper cars, batting cages, Can-Am family track
Phone (218) 829-4963
Web www.kartkountry.com

Northland Arboretum
Hiking trails, picnic area, learning center
Phone (218) 829-8770
Web http://arb.brainerd.com

This Old Farm Antique Museum
Thousands of antiques including cars, tractors, steam engines, also sawmill, blacksmith shop, shingle mill, log house, one-room school house, old time saloon and sweet shop
Phone (218) 764-2524
Web www.thisoldfarm.net

Cass County

Pillsbury State Forest
Camping, swimming, fishing, picnicking, 1 mile nature trail.
Phone (218) 825-3075

Crosby

Croft Mine Historical Park
Take a narrated ride into the simulated depths of a mine, entrance to local bike trails at end of parking lot
Phone (218) 546-5466

Hackensack

Deep Portage Conservation Reserve
Environmental learning center, nature trails, interpretive center, between Longville and Hackensack
Phone (218) 682-2325
Email portage@uslink.net
Web www.deep-portage.org

Merrifield

River Treat
Canoeing and primitive camp grounds, shuttle service, canoe trips, from half-day to 8 days, bring your own or rent
Phone (218) 765-3172

Nisswa

Nisswa Family Fun Center
Water slides, hot tubs, rollerblade track (skate rental), snack stand, children's recreation area, heated wading pool
Phone (218) 963-3545

Pequot Lakes

Bump and Putt Family Fun
Bumper boats, mini golf, water wars, hoops, basketball, battery powered 4-wheeler track for kids
Phone (218) 568-8833

Pine River

Canoe the Pine River
Shuttle service available at Doty's RV Park and Pardner's Resort
Toll Free (800) 728-6926
Phone (218) 587-4000
Web www.pinerivermn.com

Walker

Moondance Ranch & Wildlife Park
Trail rides, pony corral, wildlife park, petting zoo, pow wows, gift shop, restaurant
Toll Free (877) 666-6526
Phone (218) 547-1055
Web www.moondanceranch.com

Willard Munger Trail

Northern Minnesota

Vital Information:

Trail Distance: 70 miles

Trail Surface: asphalt

Access Points: Hinckley, Finlayson, Willow River, Moose Lake, Carlton, Duluth

Fees and Passes: none

Trail Website: www.munger-trail.com

ABOUT THE TRAIL

The trail from Carlton to Duluth is exceptional. Smooth enough for in-line skaters, the trail passes over a steep gorge of the St. Louis River, runs along a diversion canal for the hydro-electric plant, and winds through impressive rock cuts. Hinckley, the southern terminus, is best known for the Hinckley Fire Storm of September 1, 1894. The trail follows the escape route that carried residents from town to Skunk Lake, an 18 inch deep water hole where passengers buried themselves in mud and water to escape the intense heat of the fire. For additional information, stop at the Hinckley Fire Museum in downtown.

TRAIL HIGHLIGHTS

Start in Carlton and stop a short distance later on the bridge overlooking the fast flowing waters and rocky outcrops of the St. Louis River. Further east, the trail passes a diversion canal for the hydro-electric plant, touches the northern edge of Jay Cooke State Park, passes through impressive rock cuts and offers a view of Duluth Harbor, then drops down to water level. The eastern edge is a short distance from the Lake Superior Zoo, a favorite stopping point for kids and adults alike. If you have time, try the Alex Laveau Memorial Trail from Carlton to Wrenshall, a pretty little trail with rock cuts, creeks and Jay Cooke State Park all in less than 3 miles.

ABOUT THE ROADS

The roads near the southern half of the trail are nearly as flat as the trail.

Traffic is moderate around Sandstone, less as you get further north. Highway 61 runs parallel to the trail from Hinckley to Carlton. A decent alternate to the trail, but because both the trail and the road run through a flat, monotonous landscape, they are hard to get excited about. The northern roads are much more interesting.

ROAD HIGHLIGHTS

Branch out from Wrenshall for quiet, rolling hills and a scenic loop around Chub Lake. Highway 210 through Jay Cooke is very pretty, very hilly, and sometimes busy with park traffic. Sandstone's attractive business district has a pleasant feel with its village park and brick buildings. The loop around Sturgeon Lake hugs the shoreline for a couple of miles, then heads out into the country before coming back to town. A short out and back on Highway 46 will give the best lake views. A combination of roads with paved shoulders connects with a trail through Moose Lake State Park near Moose Lake.

HOW TO GET THERE

Carlton is east of Interstate 35 on Highway 210, about 15 miles from Duluth. To get to the West Duluth trailhead, take Interstate 35 to Highway 23 in West Duluth and go southwest. See city map for details. Hinckley is about 70 miles south of Duluth on Interstate 35. Take Highway 48 west from I-35 to Highway 61. See trail map for details to the trailhead. All other points can be accessed by following Highway 61. See trail map.

Northern Minnesota **Willard Munger Trail**
Hinckley to Sturgeon Lake 27 miles

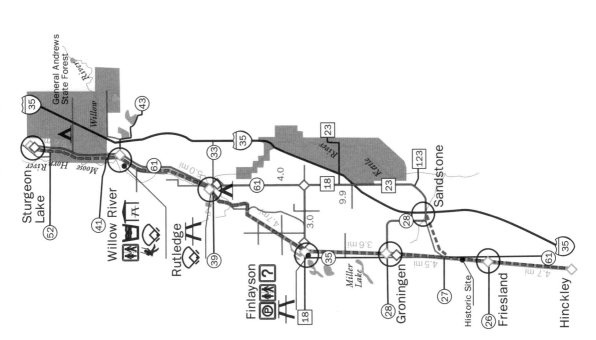

Sturgeon Lake

General Andrews State Forest

35

43

52

41

Willow River

Rutledge

39

33

35

61

25.0 mi

Willow River

Moose River

Horn River

Willow

River

23

123

Sandstone

Kettle River

23

18

61

4.0

9.9

28

Finlayson

18

3.0

4.7 mi

35

Miller Lake

28

Groningen

27

Historic Site

26

Friesland

61

35

Hinckley

3.6 mi

4.5 mi

4.7 mi

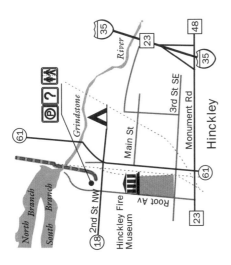

N · E · S · W

Grindstone River

North Branch

South Branch

35

23

48

35

Main St

3rd St SE

Monument Rd

Hinckley

61

61

23

18

2nd St NW

Hinckley Fire Museum

Root Av

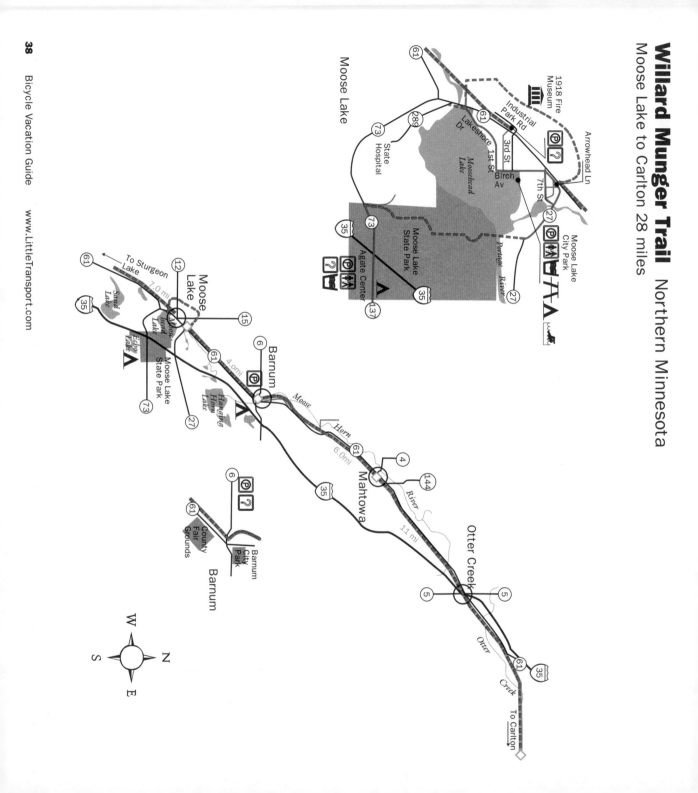

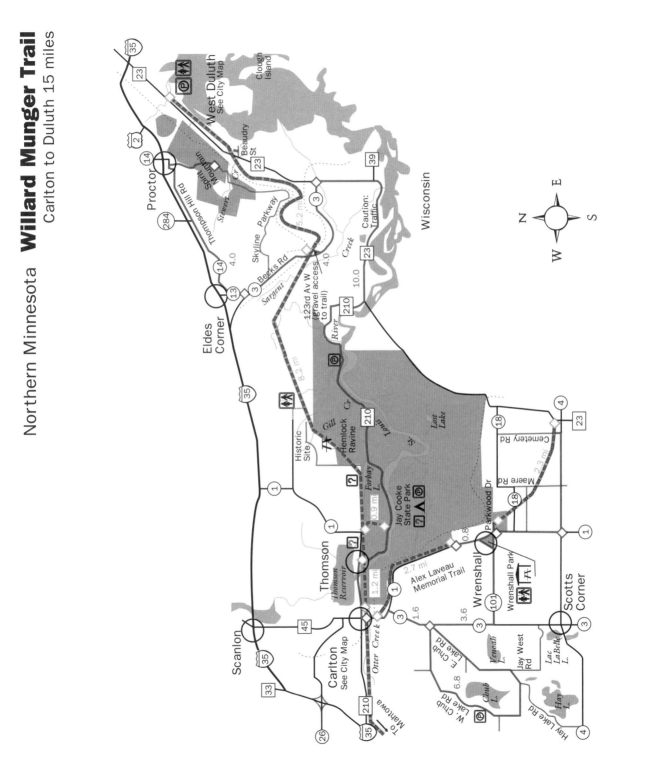

Northern Minnesota **Willard Munger Trail**
Carlton to Duluth 15 miles

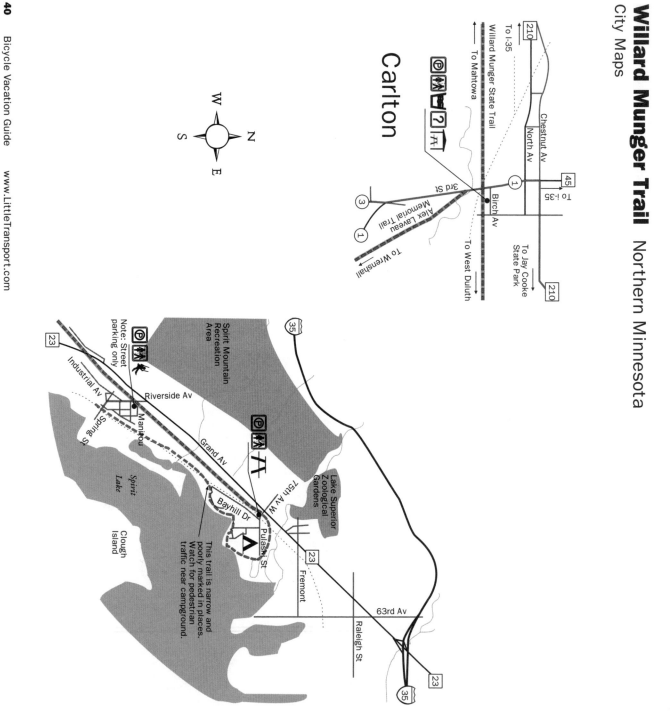

Carlton

Willard Munger State Trail

To Mahtowa

To I-35

Chestnut Av

North Av

3rd St

Alex Laveau Memorial Trail

Birch Av

To Trenshall

To West Duluth

To Jay Cooke State Park

To I-35

Spirit Mountain Recreation Area

Note: Street parking only

Industrial Av

Riverside Av

Spring St

Manitou

Grand Av

Spirit Lake

Clough Island

Bayhill Dr

75th Av W

Pulaski St

Lake Superior Zoological Gardens

Fremont

63rd Av

Raleigh St

This trail is narrow and poorly marked in places. Watch for pedestrian traffic near campground.

Willard Munger Trail

Northern Minnesota

TOURIST INFORMATION

Carlton Chamber of Commerce and Public Library
Phone (218) 384-3322

Cloquet/Carlton County Chamber of Commerce
Toll Free (800) 554-4350
Phone (218) 879-1551
Web www.cloquet.com

Duluth Convention and Visitors Bureau
Toll Free (800) 438-5884
Phone (218) 722-4011
Email cvb@visitduluth.com
Web www.visitduluth.com

Finlayson City Hall
Phone (320) 233-6472
Email finlayson@pinenet.com
Web www.ci.finlayson.mn.us

Hinckley Convention and Visitors Bureau
Toll Free (800) 996-4566
Phone (320) 384-0126
Web www.hinckleymn.com

Moose Lake Chamber of Commerce
Toll Free (800) 635-3680
Phone (218) 485-4145
Email mlchambr@lct2.net
Web www.mooselake-mn.com

Munger Trail Towns Association
Toll Free (888) 263-0586
Web www.munger-trail.com

Sandstone Chamber of Commerce
Phone (320) 245-2271

Willow River City Hall
Phone (218) 372-3137
Email cityofwr@citlink.net
Web www.ci.willow-river.mn.us

LODGING

Motels/Resorts

Barnum
Northwoods Motel & Cottages
3716 Main Street
Toll Free (800) 228-6951
Phone (218) 389-6951

Carlton
AmericInn Motel
Hwy 210 & I-35
Toll Free (800) 634-3444
Phone (218) 384-3535
Fax (218) 384-3870

Royal Pines Motel
Hwy 210 and I-35
Toll Free (800) 788-9622
Phone (218) 384-4242

Duluth
AmericInn Motel & Suites
185 Highway 2
Toll Free (800) 960-2767
Phone (218) 624-1026
Fax (218) 624-2818
Email amerdul@uslink.net
Web www.americinn.com

Spirit Mountain Travelodge
9315 Westgate Blvd.
Toll Free (800) 777-8530
Phone (218) 628-3691
Web www.duluth.com/travelodge

Finlayson
Banning Junction North Country Inn
60671 Hwy 23, I-35 Exit 195
Phone (320) 245-5284
Web www.banningjunction.com

Hinckley
Days Inn
I-35, Exit #183
Toll Free (800) 559-8951
Phone (320) 384-7751
Web www.daysinn.com

Moose Lake
AmericInn Lodge & Suites
400 Park Place Drive
Toll Free (800) 634-3444
Phone (218) 485-8885
Web www.americinn.com

Bed and Breakfast

Duluth
A.G. Thomson House
2617 East Third Street
Toll Free (877) 807-8077
Phone (218) 724-3464
Email info@thomsonhouse.biz
Web www.thomsonhouse.biz

Willard Munger Trail

Northern Minnesota

The Firelight Inn
2211 East Third Street
Toll Free (888) 724-0273
Phone (218) 724-0272
Email info@firelightinn.com
Web www.firelightinn.com

Hinckley
Dakota Lodge B&B
40497 State Hwy 48
Phone (320) 384-6052
Web www.dakotalodge.com

Camping

Carlton
Jay Cook State Park Campground
500 Highway 210 E.
Phone (218) 384-4610
Web www.dnr.state.mn.us

Moose Lake
Gafvert State Forest Campground
Forester
Rt. 2, 701 S. Kenwood
Phone (218) 485-5400

Moose Lake City Campground
PO Box 870
Phone (218) 485-4761

Moose Lake State Park Campground
4252 County Rd 137
Toll Free (888) 646-6367
Phone (218) 485-5420

Red Fox Campground & RV Park
PO Box 925
Phone (763) 286-0733

Willow River State Forest Campground
Rt2, 701 S. Kenwood

Sandstone
Banning Junction State Park
PO Box 643
Phone (320) 245-5273
Web www.dnr.state.mn.us

Sturgeon Lake
Timberline Campground
9152 Timberline Rd
Phone (218) 372-3272

GROCERIES

Carlton
Woodland Foods
(218) 384-9910

Hinckley
Daggett's Supervalu Foods
(320) 384-6185

Sandstone
Chris' Food Center
(320) 245-2229

BIKE RENTAL

Duluth
Willard Munger Inn
Toll Free (800) 982-2453
Phone (218) 624-4814
Web www.mungerinn.com

BIKE REPAIR

Duluth
Boreal Bicycle Works
Phone (218) 722-9291
Email thebrynster47@hotmail.com

Ski Hut
Phone (218) 624-5889
Fax (218) 624-5955
Web www.theskihut.com

Stewart's Bikes and Sports
Phone (218) 724-5101
Fax (218) 724-8372
Email stewarts.duluth@juno.com
Web www.stewartsbikesandsports.com

Twin Ports Cyclery
Toll Free (800) 430-0106
Phone (218) 624-4008

Sandstone
True Value
Phone (320) 245-2325

Northern Minnesota

Willard Munger Trail

FESTIVALS AND EVENTS

Barnum

August

Carleton County Fair
Exhibits, displays, talent show, horse races, demolition derby, games, rides. Check web site for dates.
Phone (218) 389-6737
Web www.carltoncountyfair.com

Duluth

May

Memorial Day Parade
Along Grand Ave in West Duluth
Toll Free (800) 438-5884
Phone (218) 722-4011

June

Grandma's Marathon
26 miles, Third Saturday.
Phone (218) 727-0947
Web www.grandmasmarathon.com

MS 150 Bike Tour
Duluth to Anoka, three day event, See Hinckley

Park Point Art Fair
Fine arts and crafts exhibitions by regional artists and artisans, recreation area at Park Point, Fourth Weekend
Toll Free (800) 438-5884

Phone (715) 398-5970
Web www.parkpoint.org

July

Fourth Fest
Food, arts and crafts, nationally known music groups, fireworks, Bayfront Festival Park
Toll Free (800) 438-5884
Phone (218) 722-4011

August

Bayfront Blues Festival
Blues and jazz bands play all weekend in open air concerts, food vendors and beer garden, Bayfront Festival Park, Second Weekend
Toll Free (800) 438-5884
Phone (715) 394-6831
Web www.bayfrontblues.com

International Folk Festival
Celebration of multi-culturalism through music, food, arts and crafts, Leif Erickson Park, First Weekend
Toll Free (800) 438-5884
Phone (218) 722-7425

Finlayson

July

July 4th Celebration
Street dance, parade, coronation, fireworks, music, games, boat parade,

July 3rd and 4th
Phone (320) 233-6472

Hinckley

June

MS 150 Bike Tour
Overnights in Hinckley at West Side Park, music, entertainment, food vendors, City wide garage sale, Second Weekend
Toll Free (800) 582-5296
Phone (612) 335-7900
Web www.nationalmssociety.org/mn

July

Annual Grand Celebration Powwow
More than 1000 dancers, singers, and drummers from throughout the Western Hemisphere compete for cash prizes, held at Powwow Grounds adjacent to Grand Casino Hinckley, Third Weekend
Toll Free (800) 472-6321
Phone (320) 384-7777
Web www.grandcasinomn.com

Corn and Clover Carnival
Grand parade, kiddie parade, pageant, talent show, pedal tractor pull, food and entertainment, antique appraisals, midway rides and games, First Weekend after the 4th
Toll Free (800) 996-4566
Phone (320) 384-7837

August

MS S.U.N. 75
In-line skating event, Hinckley to Duluth, two days on the trail, overnight in Moose Lake, First Weekend
Toll Free (800) 582-5296
Phone (612) 335-7900
Web www.nationalmssociety.org/mn

Willard Munger Trail
Northern Minnesota

FESTIVALS AND EVENTS cont'd

Moose Lake

July

4th of July Carnival
Pancake breakfast, kiddy races, parade, coronation, fireworks
Toll Free (800) 635-3680
Phone (218) 485-4145
Web www.mooselake-mn.com

Agate Days
Gem and mineral show, sponsored by the Moose Lake Historical Society, hunt for agates and quarters along Main Street, First Weekend
Toll Free (800) 635-3680
Phone (218) 485-4327
Web www.mooselake-mn.com

August

Community Night on the Trail
Kids' games, music, trail run, luminaries, Sponsored by Moose Lake Historical Society, mid-week evening in mid-August, call for exact date
Toll Free (800) 635-3680
Phone (218) 369-6090
Web www.mooselake-mn.com

Sandstone

July

Lions Club Pig Roast & Garage Sale
City wide garage/sidewalk sales and fund raising pig roast, Third Weekend
Phone (320) 245-5241

August

Quarry Days
Quarry tours, exhibits, parade, bingo, food stands, children's games, street dance, Second Weekend
Phone (320) 245-5127
Web www.sandstone.govoffice.com

October

Taste of Sandstone
Ethnic food, plane rides, fall bazaar, quilt and historic displays, quarry tours, logging, geology, and local history, Sandstone Elementary School & History and Art Center, First Weekend
Phone (320) 245-5241
Web www.sandstone.govoffice.com

Willow River

July

Willow River Days
Coronation, parade, run, softball tournament, dances, food stands, Fourth Weekend
Phone (218) 372-3733
Web www.ci.willow-river.mn.us

ALTERNATE ACTIVITIES

Carleton

Superior White Water Raft Tours
Professionally guided raft tours on the St. Louis River, minimum age 12
Phone (218) 384-4637
Web www.minnesotawhitewater.com

Finkes' Berry Farm
Pick your own strawberries in July and blueberries in August
Phone (218) 384-4432

Jay Cooke State Park
Camping, interpretive programs, bike and horse trails, hike on part of the Grand Portage of the St. Louis River

Phone (218) 384-4610
Web www.dnr.state.mn.us

Minnestalgia Winery
Outside McGregor, open for tastes and tours, seven days a week
Toll Free (866) 768-2533
Phone (218) 768-2533
Email minnestalgiawinery@citlink.net
Web /www.minnestalgia.com/

Duluth

Berry Pine Farms
Pick your own raspberries and strawberries, jams and jellies for sale
Phone (218) 721-3250

Glensheen
Tour the historic Congdon Mansion
Toll Free (888) 454-4536
Phone (218) 726-8910
Fax (218) 726-8911
Email glen@d.umn.edu
Web www.d.umn.edu/glen

Great Lakes Aquarium
Fresh water aquarium with over thirty interactive exhibits.
Phone (218) 740-3474
Fax (218) 740-2020
Email info@glaquarium.org
Web www.glaquarium.org

Lake Superior Marine Museum and Visitor Center
Film shows, model ships, and exhibits, next to Aerial Lift Bridge
Phone (218) 727-2497
Fax (218) 720-5270
Email info@lsmma.com
Web www.lsmma.com

Lake Superior Zoological Gardens
Home to more than 25 endangered and threatened species from around the world, near West Duluth trailhead
Phone (218) 733-3777
Email info@lszoo.org
Web http://www.lszoo.org

North Shore Scenic Railroad
Narrated rides on vintage trains, excursions range from romantic to family fun
Toll Free (800) 423-1273
Phone (218) 722-1273
Email nssr@cpinternet.com
Web www.lsrm.org

St. Louis County Heritage and Art Center
Four museums under one roof, Lake Superior Railroad Museum, Duluth Children's Museum, St. Louis County Historical Society, Duluth Art Institute, Duluth Playhouse and Duluth Symphony.
Toll Free (888) 733-5833
Phone (218) 727-8025
Web www.duluthdepot.org

Hinckley
Hinckley Fire Museum
Interprets great fire of 1894 through artifacts, testimony, and video, two blocks from the trailhead
Phone (320) 384-7338

St. Croix State Park
Camping, swimming, hiking, biking, fishing
Phone (320) 384-6591
Web www.dnr.state.mn.us

Moose Lake
Moose Lake City Beach
Swimming, fishing pier, camping
Phone (218) 485-4761

Sandstone
Audubon Center of the North Woods
Residential environmental learning center and retreat on the shores of Grindstone Lake: 535 acre sanctuary, with hiking and learning environments.
Toll Free (888) 404-7743
Phone (320) 824-5264
Email audubon1@audubon-center.org
Web www.audubon-center.org

Banning State Park
Canoeing, hiking, kayaking, ice cave, quarry ruins, Wolf Creek Falls
Phone (320) 245-2668
Web www.dnr.state.mn.us

Sandstone History and Art Center
Diorama of Sandstone Quarry, historical artifacts, rotating art exhibits
Phone (320) 245-2131
Email shaac@ubetnet.com

Scanlon
River Inn
Summer launch site on St. Louis River for Superior White Water Rafting Tours.
Phone (218) 384-4637
Web www.minnesotawhitewater.com

Central Lakes Trail

Vital Information:

Trail Distance: 38 miles

Trail Surface: asphalt

Access Points: Osakis, Nelson, Alexandria, Garfield, Ashby, Dalton, Fergus Falls

Fees and Passes: none

Trail Website:
www.CentralLakesTrail.com

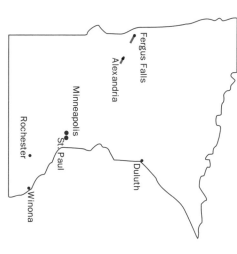

ABOUT THE TRAIL

Two trails planning to merge with each other, then to the Lake Wobegon Trail. They run through a unique part of Minnesota, where prairie and hardwood forest meet, and they reflect that variety. The trails run through a scenic blend of lakes, prairie potholes, open farmland and wooded lots, with small towns at seven to ten mile intervals. These are very quiet trails with little highway noise. The pavement is new and smooth enough for in-line skates.

TRAIL HIGHLIGHTS

Osakis to Alexandria: Start in Alexandria, the heart of the woodlands and lakes area. Going west, you'll cross a number of channels and culverts connecting lakes. The channels are popular for swimming, boating and fishing. The further you get east and west of Alexandria, the more open the land becomes. You'll see lots of prairie potholes; small shallow lakes with cattails and wetland grasses, but few trees. Ashby to Fergus Falls: Stop in Dalton and wander the grounds of the Lake Regions Threshermen's Show. The old farm machinery and scale model railroad are worth seeing even if the festival isn't in full swing. Ignore the trailhead at Hwy 210 in Fergus Falls unless you are an in-line skater. The trailhead is behind self storage garages and has no facilities. Bicyclists will want to start at Delagoon Park just south of Fergus Falls. The park has complete facilities and is easy to find. Access from the park to the trail is via a hard

packed gravel trail. OK for bicyclists, but very difficult for skaters.

ABOUT THE ROADS

The roads take advantage of the rolling terrain and give a nice perspective on the variety of land and its uses in the area. You'll see woodlots, farms, lakes and potholes, sometimes from high above, at other times from lake level. Traffic is low to moderate.

ROAD HIGHLIGHTS

The northern route from Fergus Falls to Dalton follows the very pretty Otter Tail County Scenic Byway. This is a roller coaster ride with non-stop climbs and dips, some long, but not exceptionally steep. The road flattens somewhat between Dalton and Hwy 117 where it connects to the trail just west of Ashby. Very low traffic and nice scenery.

HOW TO GET THERE

Alexandria is about 50 miles west of St. Cloud on I-94. Take the Hwy 29 exit and go north. See City Map of Alexandria for details to trail. Fergus Falls is about 50 miles west of Alexandria and 55 east of Fargo/Moorhead on I-94. Take the Hwy 210 exit. See City Map of Fergus Falls for Trailhead access.

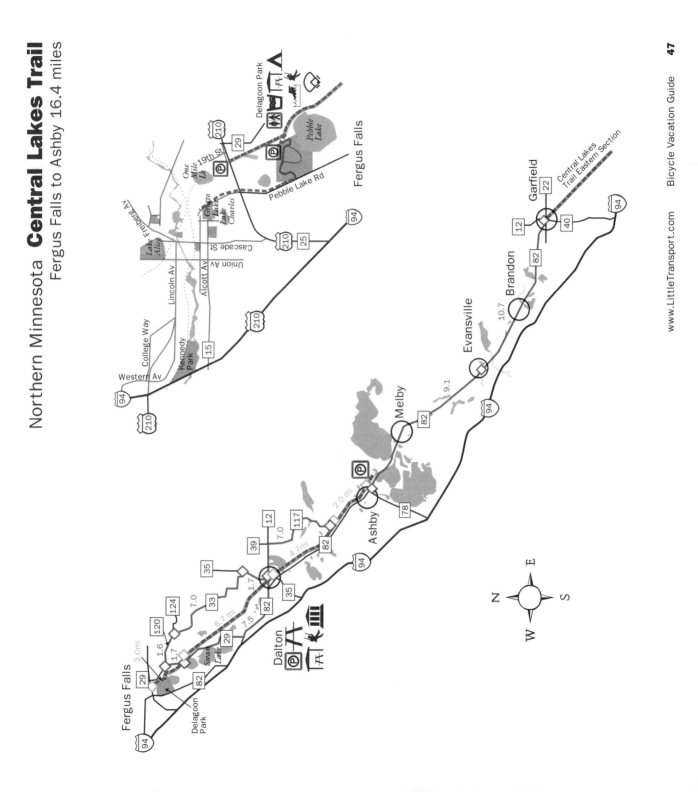

Northern Minnesota **Central Lakes Trail**
Fergus Falls to Ashby 16.4 miles

Delagoon Park

210

29

Pebble Lake

Fergus Falls

One Mile U.

19th St.

Pebble Lake Rd

Grotto Lake

Lake Charles

Fletcher Av

210

25

Cascade St

Union Av

Alcott Av

Lake Alice

Lincoln Av

College Way

Kennedy Park

Western Av

94

210

94

210

Garfield

22

Central Lakes Trail Eastern Section

12

40

94

82

Brandon

10.7

Evansville

9.1

82

94

Melby

82

2.0 mi

Ashby

78

94

12

117

82

39

7.0

4.7mi

35

1.7

33

124

7.0

82

35

6.7 mi

7.5

120

1.6

1.7

29

82

3.0mi

Fergus Falls

Swan Lake

Delagoon Park

94

Dalton

N E S W

Central Lakes Trail Northern Minnesota
Garfield to Lake Osakis 16.7 miles

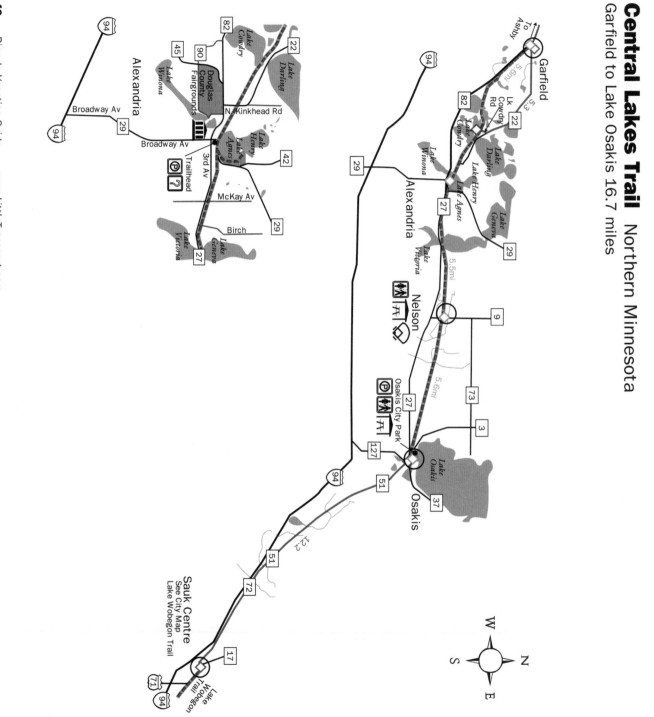

To Ashby

Garfield

5.6mi

5.3

82

Lk Cowdry Rd

22

94

Lake Cowdry

Lake Darling

Lake Winona

Lake Henry

Lake Geneva

Lake Agnes

27

Alexandria

Lake Victoria

29

5.5mi

Nelson

9

73

5.6mi

27

3

Osakis City Park

127

94

51

Lake Osakis

Osakis

37

12.2

51

72

Sauk Centre
See City Map
Lake Wobegon Trail

17

71

94

Lake Wobegon Trail

N
W   E
S

Alexandria (inset)

94

82

Lake Cowdry

45   90

22

Lake Darling

Alexandria

Douglas County Fairgrounds

Lake Winona

N. Kinkhead Rd

29

Broadway Av

Broadway Av

3rd Av

Trailhead

42

Lake Agnes

Lake Henry

McKay Av

29

Birch

Lake Victoria

27

Lake Geneva

94

Alexandria Lakes Area Chamber of Commerce
Toll Free (800) 235-9441
Phone (320) 763-3161
Email alexrecr@rea-alp.com
Web www.alexandriamn.org

Central Lakes Trail
Toll Free (800) 422-0785
Web www.CentralLakesTrail.com

Fergus Falls Area Chamber of Commerce
Phone (218) 736-6951
Email chamber@prtel.com
Web www.fergusfalls.com

Fergus Falls Convention & Visitors Bureau
Toll Free (800) 726-8959
Phone (218) 739-0125
Email cvb@cpinternet.com
Web www.visitfergusfalls.com

Lake Osakis Resort Association
Toll Free (800) 422-0785
Web http://lakeosakismn.com

LODGING

Motels/Resorts
Alexandria

AmericInn
4520 Highway 29 S
Toll Free (800) 634-3444
Phone (320) 763-6808
Web www.americinn.com

Broken Arrow Resort
3408 State Highway 27 E
Toll Free (800) 729-2202
Phone (320) 763-4646
Email see website
Web www.brokenarrowresort.com

Butch & Nev's Resort
1810 Geneva Road
Phone (320) 762-0898

Days Inn
4810 Highway 29 S
Toll Free (800) 329-7466
Phone (320) 762-1171
Web www.daysinn.com

Holiday Inn
5637 State Highway 29 S
Toll Free (800) 465-4329
Phone (320) 763-6577

L Motel
910 Highway 27 W
Toll Free (800) 733-1793
Phone (320) 763-5121
Email lmotel@rea-alp.com
Web www.rea-alp.com/~lmotel

Lazy Day Resort
250 Three Havens Dr NE
Toll Free (888) 850-4569
Phone (320) 846-1161

Lilac Lodge Resort
114 Lilac Lodge Road
Toll Free (877) 335-0263
Phone (320) 763-4440

Shady Lawn Resort
1321 S. Darling Dr NW
Phone (320) 763-3559

Skyline Motel
605 30th Ave W
Toll Free (800) 467-4096
Phone (320) 763-3175

Sun Valley Resort & Campground
10045 State Highway 27 W
Phone (320) 886-5417
Fax (320) 886-5217
Email sunvaley@rea-alp.com
Web www.alexandriamn.com/sunvalley

Super 8 Motel
4620 Highway 29 S
Toll Free (800) 800-8000
Phone (320) 763-6552
Web www.super8.com

Vacationer's Inn
1327 W Lake Cowdry Rd NW
Phone (320) 763-5011
Web www.alexweb.net/vacationersinn

Val Halla Villa
1301 S Darling Dr NW
Phone (320) 763-5869

Viking Trail Resort
2301 County Road 22 NW
Phone (320) 763-3602

Fergus Falls

Jewel Motel
1602 Pebble Lake Rd
Phone (218) 739-5430

Lakeland Motel
1912 Pebble Lake Rd
Phone (218) 736-6938

Swan Lake Resort
17463 County Highway 29
Toll Free (800) 697-4626
Phone (218) 736-4626
Email swanlk@prtel.com
Web www.swanlkresort.com

Osakis

Idlewilde Resort
Box 299B
811 Lake St.
Toll Free (800) 648-1713
Phone (320) 859-2135
Email idlewild@midwestinfo.net
Web www.idlewilde.com

Lakeland Motel
204 W Nokomis St
Phone (320) 859-4466
Email BHold@webtv.net

Midway Beach Resort/Campground
1821 Lake Street E
Toll Free (800) 367-2547
Phone (320) 859-4410
Email midwaybr@midwaybeach.com
Web www.midwaybeach.com

Bed and Breakfast

Alexandria

Cedar Rose Inn
422 7th Ave W
Toll Free (888) 203-5333
Phone (320) 762-8430
Web http://www.cedarroseinn.com
Lake Le Homme Dieu B&B
441 S Le Homme Dieu Dr NE

Toll Free (800) 943-5875
Phone (320) 846-5875
Email sjradj@rea-alp.com
Web www.llbedandbreakfast.com

Pillars Bed & Breakfast
1004 Elm St
Toll Free (866) 336-5682
Phone (320) 762-2700
Email pillarbb@rea-alp.com
Web http://www.pillarsbandb.itgo.com

Ashby

Harvest Inn B & B
200 Melby Ave
Phone (218) 747-2334
Email info@harvestinn.net
Web www.harvestinn.net

Fergus Falls

Bakketopp Hus Bed & Breakfast
20571 Hillcrest Road
Toll Free (800) 739-2915
Phone (218) 739-2915
Email ddn@prtel.com
Web www.bbonline.com/mn

Russell's Family B&B
506 Union Ave. S
Phone (218) 736-6220

Osakis

Just Like Grandma's B&B
113 West Main
Phone (320) 859-4504

Lake Street B&B
204 Lake Street East
P.O. Box 297
Phone (320) 859-3847
Email jccarp@miswestinfo.net

Camping

Alexandria

Sun Valley Resort & Campground
10045 State Highway 27 W
Phone (320) 886-5417
Fax (320) 886-5217
Email sunvaley@rea-alp.com
Web www.alexandriamn.com/sunvalley

Garfield

Oak Park Kampground
10196 County Road 8 NW
Phone (320) 834-2345

Osakis

Midway Beach Resort/Campground
1821 Lake Street E
Toll Free (800) 367-2547
Phone (320) 859-4410
Email midwaybr@midwestinfo.net
Web www.midwaybeach.com

Northern Minnesota **Central Lakes Trail**

GROCERIES

Alexandria

Elden's Food Fair
(320) 763-3446

Pete's Country Market
(320) 762-1158

Ashby

Anderson Foods
(218) 747-2660

Fergus Falls

BJ's East
(218) 736-3401

Lakeway Market
(218) 736-7977

Service Foods Supervalu
(218) 998-9000

Garfield

Cenex Convenience Store
(320) 834-2224

Nelson

Jill's Gas & Grocery
(320) 763-6029

Osakis

Jim's Home Quality Foods Inc
(320) 859-2194

BIKE RENTAL

Alexandria

The Bike & Fitness Company
Phone (320) 762-8493

BIKE REPAIR

Alexandria

Bike Shop
Phone (320) 762-8493

FESTIVALS AND EVENTS

Alexandria

May

Awake the Lakes
Kick off summer featuring a street dance, beer garden, carnival and children's activities throughout town.
Memorial Day Weekend
Toll Free (800) 235-9441
Phone (320) 763-3161
Web www.alexandriamn.org

Chain of Lakes Sprint Triathlon
Swim 600 yards. Bike 14 miles. Run 3.5 miles. First Saturday
Phone (320) 529-0884
Web www.pickleevents.com/colt

June

Vikingland Band Festival
Minnesota's premiere high school marching competition. Last Sunday
Toll Free (800) 235-9441
Phone (320) 763-3161
Web http://www.marching.com

July

4th of July Fireworks
Fireworks food and musical entertainment on the lakeside lawn of Arrowwood Resort along Lake Darling
Toll Free (866) 386-5263
Phone (320) 762-1124
Web www.arrowwoodresort.com

Art in the Park
City Park is transformed into a marketplace of crafters, musicians, and artists from across the country. Plus music, live entertainment and food.
Call for date.
Toll Free (800) 235-9441
Phone (320) 763-3161

August

Douglas County Fair
4-H exhibits, business exhibits, stock car racing, food vendors, entertainment and the midway. Call for dates.
Phone (320) 834-4796

Central Lakes Trail Northern Minnesota

September

Grape Stomp & Fall Festival
Carlos Creek Winery, 6693 County
Road 34 NW. Tour the Winery, stables,
apple orchard & maze. 100 wine, food
& craft booths, live music, I Love Lucy
contest, Call for date.
Phone (320) 846-5443
Web www.carloscreekwinery.com

Dalton

September

Lake Region Pioneer Threshing
Historic farm machinery and French
locomotive from World Wars I and II.
Threshing demonstrations, horse pulls,
tractor pulls, sawing demos, home-
maker demos parade and entertain-
ment. First weekend after Labor Day
Toll Free (800) 726-8959
Phone (218) 736-6505
Web www.visitfergusfalls.com

Fergus Falls

May

Pedal De Ponds Bike Tour
Choose from 100K, 50K, 100 mile, 20
mile rides. Sag wagon, refreshment
stops on the route. First Saturday.
Phone (218) 739-4489

June

Lincoln Avenue Fine Arts Festival
Display booths of artists' work, juried
exhibition. Hands on visual arts activi-
ties for children, folk music, writers'
workshop and other performances.
Second full weekend
Phone (218) 736-5453
Web www.fergusarts.org

SummerFest
Kids activities, parade, art & craft
sale. Second full weekend

Phone (218) 736-6951
Web www.fergusfalls.com

July

Hoot Lake Triathalon
Hoot Lake Public Access: Swim .25
mile open water in Hoot Lake. Bike 16
miles on rolling hills. 3 Mile Run. Check
website for date
Phone (218) 736-4825
Web http://www.pickleevents.com
West Otter Tail County Fair
Thursday through Sunday, Third
Weekend
Web www.otcfair.com

Osakis

June

Osakis Festival
Flea market, craft sale, food vendors,
parades, pony rides, petting zoo, sand
pile money hunt, music, fire depart-
ment water fight, at the City Park
Call for date.
Toll Free (800) 422-0785
Phone (320) 859-3777
Web http://lakeosakismn.com

July

4th of July Fireworks
At the Osakis Country Club golf course
Toll Free (800) 422-0785
Phone (320) 859-3777
Web http://lakeosakismn.com

August

Grammafest
Music, food and displays, crafts,
demonstrations and entertainment,
Second Weekend
Toll Free (800) 422-0785
Phone (320) 859-3777
Web http://lakeosakismn.com

Alexandria

Casey's Amusement Park
3 great tracks-naskarts, indy karts,
family and kiddie karts, bumper boats,
mini-golf, batting cages, picnic area
Phone (320) 763-7576
Fax (320) 834-5289

Horseback Riding
Arrowwood Resort Guided Trail and
Pony Rides
Toll Free (866) 386-5263
Phone (320) 762-1124
Web www.arrowwoodresort.com

Runestone Museum
Enjoy the story of the Kensington
Runestone, Norse history, and many
exhibits which demonstrate early pioneer and Native American life of the
1870's, Fort Alexandria's authentic
log buildings, country school house,
agriculture museum, 40 ft Viking Ship
replica, and a large rotating exhibit
which changes annually.
Phone (320) 763-3160
Fax (320) 763-9705

Email bigole@rea-alp.com
Web www.runestonemuseum.org

Theatre L'Homme Dieu
Professional summer theatre,
performances Wednesday through
Sunday, Mid June - Mid August,
Phone (320) 846-3150
Web http://www.tlhd.org

Fergus Falls

A Center for the Arts
Theatrical and musical productions,
summer children's theater, community
orchestra
Phone (218) 736-5453
Email ac4ta@prtel.com
Web www.fergusarts.org

Otter Tail County Historical Museum
Laid out in an interpretive style with a
1916 main street, wildlife exhibit,
agricultural exhibits and period rooms.
Phone (218) 736-6038
Email otchs@prtel.com
Web www.otchs.org

Prairie Wetlands Learning Center
The first residential environmental
education center operated by the U.S.
Fish and Wildlife Service. Focuses on
the understanding of prairies and wetlands. 325 acres of native and
restored prairie, wetlands and 4.5
miles of trails. The Visitor Center
houses a 2500 square foot exhibit
area and the Bluestem Store.
Phone (218) 736-0938
Fax (218) 736-0941
Email prairiewet@fws.gov
Web http://midwest.fws.gov/pwlc

Lake Wobegon Trail

Vital Information:

Trail Distance: 47 miles

Trail Surface: asphalt

Access Points: Sauk Centre, Melrose, Freeport, Albany, Avon, Holdingford, St. Joseph

Fees and Passes: none

Trail Website:
www.lakewobegontrails.com

ABOUT THE TRAIL

Named for the mythical town of Lake Wobegon from Garrison Keillor's "Prairie Home Companion," the trail passes through towns that could have been the model for Lake Wobegon. This is a land with deep roots in agriculture. The trail is mostly flat and wide open. Woodlands are limited to a few short stretches, so bring sunscreen. St. Joseph, on the eastern side, has the most lakes and woods near the trail. The trail comes right up to I-94 between Albany and Freeport where the noise from the freeway is quite noticeable. The new spur between Albany and Holdingford plunges deep into farm country, away from the noise and traffic of I-94. Plenty of sun at both ends of the Holdingford spur, more shade in the middle section. The trail rises slowly toward Holdingford, providing some nice views of pothole lakes.

TRAIL HIGHLIGHTS

The 15-mile stretch from Albany to St. Joseph is the most scenic part of the trail, with a mix of woods, lakes and prairie and some distance from the Interstate. The spur to Holdingford goes deep into the rural areas of Stearns County with some climbs, open areas and woods.

The churches along the trail are distinctive buildings with beautiful bell towers, and steeples. St. Mary's in Melrose is on the National Register of Historic Places, but be sure to see St. Paul's in Sauk Centre, Sacred Heart in Freeport, Seven Dolors in Albany

and the Church of St. Benedict in Avon. Memoryville, near Melrose, is a unique theme park next to the trail.

ABOUT THE ROADS

Mostly paved, low traffic roads through rolling farmland. The terrain breaks up the endless fields of crops enough to keep the routes interesting. The best roads generally skirt a lakeshore or wind along low rises.

ROAD HIGHLIGHTS

Hwy 173 south out of Melrose is a must ride, even if you only ride to Hwy 30, then turn around and ride back to town. It rises and dips as it follows a ridge with scenic views, trees and nice little twists and turns. Hwy 154, north of Albany, is a rolling twisting mix of woodlots and farm fields. Pelican Lake Road, 2 miles west of St. Anna, follows the eastern shoreline of Pelican Lake. Small lake cabins line the shore and farm fields butt up against the eastern edge of the road. Quaker Rd., east of Albany, is an excellent alternative to the trail. It's best described as quietly beautiful, rather than dramatic. A long, low grassy wetland parallels the north side of the road for miles. Tower Road, connecting Quaker with the trail, is quite hilly and scenic. Traffic is low on both roads.

HOW TO GET THERE

St. Joseph is about 8 miles west of St. Cloud on I-94. All trail towns are directly accessible from Interstate 94.

Northern Minnesota **Lake Wobegon Trail**
Avon to Sauk Centre 47 miles

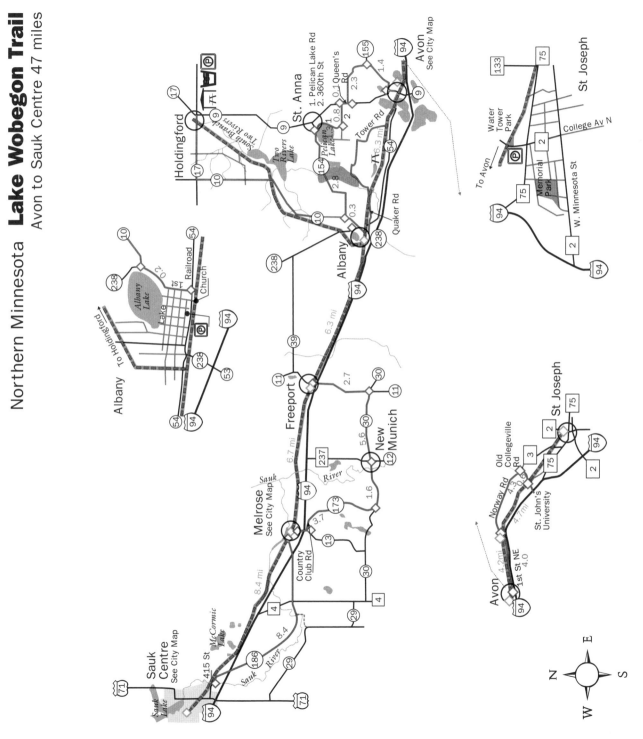

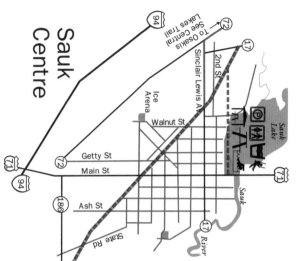

Sauk Centre

94
72
To Osakis
See Central
Lakes Trail
17
Sinclair Lewis Av
2nd St
Ice
Arena
Walnut St
Sauk Lake
71
72
Getty St
Main St
71
94
186
Ash St
State Rd
17
Sauk River

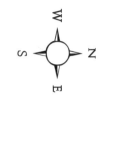

N
W
S
E

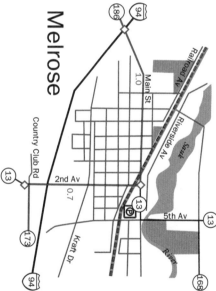

Melrose

186
94
Railroad Av
1.0
Main St
Riverside Av
Sauk
Country Club Rd
13
2nd Av
0.7
13
5th Av
13
173
Kraft Dr
94
168
River

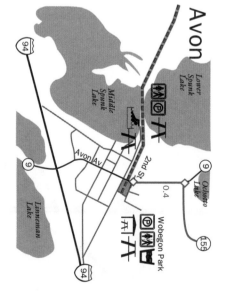

Avon

94
Lower Spunk Lake
Middle Spunk Lake
2nd St
9
Avon Av
9
0.4
Ochonzo Lake
159
94
Linneman Lake
Wobegon Park

Northern Minnesota **Lake Wobegon Trail**

Albany Area Chamber of Commerce
Phone (320) 845-7777
Fax (320) 845-2346
Email albanycc@albanytel.com
Web www.albanymnchamber.com

Avon Chamber of Commerce
Phone (320) 356-7922
Web www.avonmnchamber.com

Freeport Chamber of Commerce
Phone (320) 836-2695
Web www.freeportmn.org

Holdingford City Hall
Phone (320) 746-2966

Melrose Chamber of Commerce
Phone (320) 256-7174
Email chamber@meltel.net
Web www.melrosemn.org

Sauk Centre Chamber of Commerce
Phone (320) 352-5201
Fax (320) 352-5202
Email see website
Web www.saukcentrechamber.com

LODGING

Motels/Resorts

Sauk Centre
AmericInn Motel
1230 Timberlane Drive
Toll Free (877) 352-1199

Phone (320) 352-2800
Fax (320) 352-2800
Web www.americinnsaukcentre.com

Palmer House
Hwy 71, 1 mile north of I-94
Toll Free (866) 834-9100
Phone (320) 351-9104
Fax (632) 351-9104

Camping

Melrose
Birch Lake State Forest Campground
Charles Lindbergh State Park
PO Box 364
Phone (320) 616-2525

Riverside Park
Phone (320) 256-4278

Sauk River Park
206 N. Fifth Ave E.
Phone (320) 256-4278

Monticello
Lake Maria State Park Campground
11411 Clementa Ave. NW
Phone (612) 878-2325
Web www.dnr.state.mn.us

GROCERIES

Avon
Dahlin's Supermarket
(320) 356-7472

Freeport
Corner Store
(320) 836-2164

Melrose
Ernie's Jubilee Foods Deli
(320) 256-4444

Sauk Centre
Coborn's
(320) 352-5990

Pfeffer's Country Market
(320) 352-6490

Lake Wobegon Trail
Northern Minnesota

BIKE REPAIR

St. Cloud

Fitzharris Ski and Sport
Phone (320) 251-2844

Granite City Schwinn
Phone (320) 251-7540

Out-N-About Gear
Toll Free (800) 371-9036
Phone (320) 251-9036
Fax (320) 240-9001

Rod's Bike Shop
Phone (320) 259-1964

FESTIVALS AND EVENTS

Albany

September

Albany Pioneer Days
Tractor - steamer parade, old fashioned arts and crafts, lumber sawing, flour milling, blacksmith shop, model railroad museum, flea market, Check web site for dates.
Phone (320) 845-7777
Web www.albanymnchamber.com

Heritage Day
Saturday only, two parades, firefighters water fight, beer garden, food vendors, mini-carnival, fireworks, Check

web site for date.
Phone (320) 845-7777
Web www.albanymnchamber.com

Avon

All Summer

Fisher's Club
For many generations, the place to be on Friday nights for the best walleye fillets and loud, friendly conversation. On the banks of Middle Spunk Lake, Memorial Day through Labor Day

June

Spunktacular Days
Parade, water ski show, music, beer garden, carnival, 5k run, Third Weekend
Phone (320) 356-7922
Web www.avonmnchamber.com

Freeport

Freeport Craft Fair
Arts and crafts by local artists. Late Summer, See web site for details.
Phone (320) 836-2695
Web www.freeportmn.org

July

Parrish Festival
Parade, music, dance, food vendors, beer garden, kids' games, Second Weekend
Phone (320) 836-2143
Web www.freeportmn.org

Melrose

Independence Day Celebration
Parade, carnival rides, food vendors, fireworks, Sauk River Park, Friday and Saturday before the 4th of July
Phone (320) 256-7174
Web www.melrosemn.org

Sauk Centre

July

Sinclair Lewis Days
Craft sales, parade, pageant, dance, games, activities for kids, check web

site for dates.
Phone (320) 352-5201
Web www.saukcentrechamber.com

St. Joseph

July

Tour of Saints Bike Ride
Starts at College of St. Benedict and winds through beautiful central Minnesota: 50 or 35 mile route. See web site for date.
Toll Free (800) 651-8687
Phone (320) 251-9036
Web www.tourofsaints.com

ALTERNATE ACTIVITIES

Albany

North Park
Picnic area, playground
Phone (320) 845-4244
Web www.ci.albany.mn.us

ALTERNATE ACTIVITIES cont'd

Avon

Swimming beach
Beach and observation tower across from bike trail
Phone (320) 356-7922

Melrose

Birch Lake State Forest
Camping, boating, hiking trails.
Facility managed by Charles Lindbergh State Park.
Phone (320) 616-2525
Web www.dnr.state.mn.us

Jaycee Park
Picnic area, playground, close to trail
Phone (320) 256-4278
Email chamber@meltel.net
Web www.melrosemn.org

Melrose Area Historical Society
Large collection of antique memorabilia of the area, adjacent to the trail
Phone (320) 256-4996
Web www.melrosemnhistory.com

Riverside Park
Close by trail: picnic area, pavilion, camping sites, public restrooms
Phone (320) 256-4278

Sauk Centre

Sauk Centre Area Historical Society
19th century artifacts housed in the Bryant Public Library
Phone (320) 352-5201
Fax (320) 352-5202
Email see website
Web www.saukcentrechamber.com

Sinclair Lewis Museum and Boyhood Home
1880 story and a half home furnished with period furnishings, across the street from Sinclair Lewis' birthplace, Open Memorial Day to Labor Day
Phone (320) 352-5201
Email see website
Web www.saukcentrechamber.com

Sinclair Lewis Park
Shelter, picnic area, Wednesday night band concerts in the summer
Phone (320) 352-5201
Fax (320) 352-5202
Email see website
Web www.saukcentrechamber.com

Luce Line Trail

Vital Information:

Trail Distance: 24 miles

Trail Surface: limestone

Access Points: Medicine Lake Beach, 13th Ave. in Plymouth, Parker's Lake, Vicksburg Lane, Stubb's Bay Park, Watertown

Fees and Passes: none

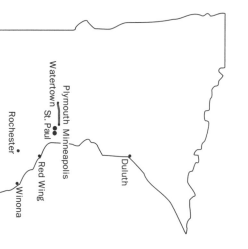

ABOUT THE TRAIL

This is the oldest and narrowest state trail. At only 6 feet wide, the trail is narrow enough to have a full canopy of leaves shading it through the summer. This is an underused trail, especially on the western edge where use is so light that grasses grow in the center of the trail, creating a jeep track appearance. The light use and lack of towns along the trail give it a remarkably remote feeling considering it starts in the West Metro area. The trail has recently been extended to East Medicine Lake Beach Park, a nice addition that takes in marshes and some heavily wooded areas.

TRAIL HIGHLIGHTS

The eastern end of the trail passes through remnants of the Big Woods and low density residential areas with large wooded lots. The woods continue as a buffer all the way to Watertown, but the land to the north and south opens into rural farmland. Numerous lakes and cattail marshes line the entire length of the trail.

ABOUT THE ROADS

Generally low traffic and smooth surfaced, the roads that parallel the trail offer a pleasant return route with medium rolling hills. Traffic is heavier near the parks on weekends and everywhere during weekday rush hour.

ROAD HIGHLIGHTS

Highway 26 is an ex-urban road with a mix of residential and farm land, low traffic, smooth surface and rolling hills. Roads in the Wayzata/Orono area pass through quiet residential streets with large houses and big lots. Wander off the beaten path for a look at some beautiful old estates. Baker Park Reserve offers a wide range of recreational facilities including swimming and bike trails. Highway 19 to the Park Reserve is generally low traffic and wide, but can get crowded with vehicles going to the Park. Lake Rebecca is another great park, but traffic is heavier on routes to the park. For more route information in this area, pick up a copy of the Twin Cities Bike Map by Little Transport Press.

HOW TO GET THERE

The eastern trailhead begins at East Medicine Lake Beach Park. Take Hwy 169 to the 13th Ave/Plymouth Ave Exit. Go north on Kilmer, a frontage road that runs up the western side of Hwy 169, to 17th Ave. N. Turn left and go to the beach. Parker Lake and Vicksburg Lane access points get you either, go west on Highway 6. See city map for details. Watertown, the western terminus, can be reached by taking Highway 12 west to Delano, then take Highways 16/27 south. See trail map for details on access to Watertown and other points along the trail.

Central Minnesota Luce Line Trail
Medicine Lake to Watertown 24 miles

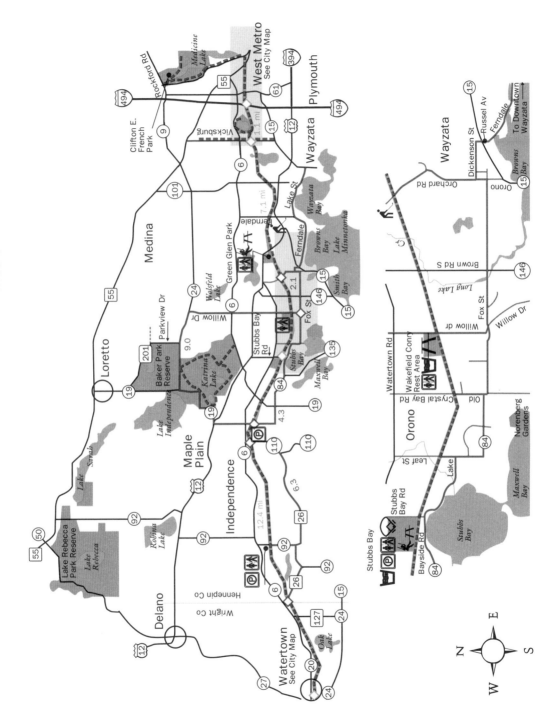

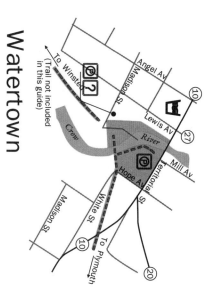

Luce Line Trail Central Minnesota
City Maps

Watertown

Plymouth

Medicine Lake

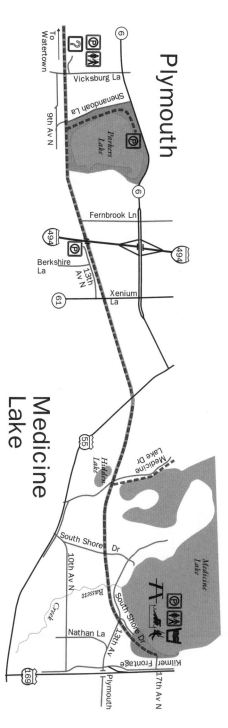

Central Minnesota **Luce Line Trail**

TOURIST INFORMATION

City of Maple Plain
Phone (763) 479-0515
Email cityhall@mapleplain.com
Web www.mapleplain.com

DNR Trails and Waterways Area Office
Phone (952) 826-6769
Fax (952) 826-6767
Web www.dnr.state.mn.us

Greater Wayzata Chamber of Commerce
Phone (952) 473-9595
Fax (952) 473-6266
Email info@wayzatachamber.com
Web www.wayzatachamber.com

Long Lake Chamber of Commerce
Phone (952) 473-1329
Web www.longlake-orono.org

Northwest Suburban Chamber of Commerce
Phone (763) 420-3242
Fax (763) 420-5964
Email info@nwschamber.com
Web www.nwschamber.com

Plymouth Park and Recreation
Phone (763) 509-5200
Fax (763) 509-5207
Email recreation@ci.plymouth.mn.us
Web www2.ci.plymouth.mn.us

Watertown City Offices
Phone (952) 955-2681
Fax (952) 955-2695
Email info@ci.watertown.mn.us
Web www.ci.watertown.mn.us

LODGING

Motels/Resorts
Plymouth
Comfort Inn Plymouth
3000 Harbor Lane
Toll Free (800) 424-6423
Phone (763) 559-1222
Web www.comfortinn.com

Country Inn & Suites
210 Carlson Parkway North
Toll Free (877) 668-9330
Phone (763) 473-3008

Camping
Plymouth
Baker Park Reserve
3800 Cty Rd 24
Phone (763) 559-6700
Web www.hennepinparks.org

GROCERIES

Plymouth
Cub Foods
(763) 559-2110

Rainbow Foods
(763) 541-9044

Rick's Market
(763) 473-1561

Wayzata
Lund's Food Stores
(952) 476-2223

BIKE REPAIR

Long Lake
Gear West Ski Bike Run
Toll Free (877) 874-9587
Phone (952) 473-0093
Email triclub@gearwest.com
Web www.gearwest.com

Maple Grove
Maple Grove Cycle and Fitness
Phone (763) 420-8878

Wayzata
Sports Hut
Phone (952) 473-8843
Fax (952) 473-9292
Email sptshut@aol.com
Web www.sportshut.com

FESTIVALS AND EVENTS

Long Lake
June
Buckhorn Days
Friday and Saturday historic tribute to the Buckhorn Place, fishing tournament, volleyball tournament, carnival, kids' games, music, water ski show, family fun, Fourth Weekend
Phone (952) 473-1329
Web www.longlake-orono.org

Luce Line Trail Central Minnesota

August

August

Corn Days
Corn feed, beer tent, wine tasting, food stands, children's events, music, fun run, parade, bingo, St. George Catholic Church, Second Weekend
Phone (952) 475-3739

Maple Plain

August

Polo Classic
Polo and cricket matches, pony rides, picnic, dancing, gourmet food, fund raiser for Childrens' Home Society, West End Farm, First Weekend
Phone (651) 255-2316
Web www.poloclassic.com

Watertown

July

Rails to Trails Festival
Fire muster parade, kids' games, pet parade, Taste of Watertown, food fair, fun run, Christian music festival, Check web site for dates.
Phone (952) 955-2681
Web www.ci.watertown.mn.us

Wayzata

September

James J. Hill Days
Kids' games, arts and crafts fair, food booths, parade, historical displays, antique show, dachshund races. Weekend after Labor Day
Phone (952) 473-9595
Web www.wayzatachamber.com

ALTERNATE ACTIVITIES

Long Lake
West Hennepin Pioneer Museum
Artifacts from the pioneer days, Open Saturdays, 10am to 4pm
Phone (952) 473-6557

Wolsfeld Woods
DNR Scientific and Natural Area, 185 acres with hiking trails, woodlands, blooming wildflowers in spring, Highway 6 at Brown Rd
Phone (651) 296-2835
Fax (651) 296-1811

Maple Plain
Baker Park Reserve
Fishing, swimming, hiking, picnicking, play area, concessions, bike trail
Phone (763) 476-4666
Email see website
Web www.threeriversparkdistrict.org

Homestead Orchard
Apple blossom wagon rides, fall raspberries and apple picking, picnic table, hayrides, petting zoo, pumpkin patch and observation beehive, Check web site for more information.
Phone (763) 479-2448
Web www.mnhomesteadorchard.com

Orono
Wood-Rill
400 year old growth forest, DNR Scientific & Natural Area located on Old Long Lake Rd
Phone (651) 296-2835

Plymouth
Clifton E. French Park
Fishing, swimming, hiking, picnicking, play area, concessions, bike trail
Phone (763) 559-8891
Email see website
Web www.threeriversparkdistrict.org

Severs Farm Market and Corn Maze
Seasonal summer produce, pick your own pumpkins, corn maze mid-August to Halloween
Phone (763) 974-5000
Web www.severscornmaze.com

Rockford
Lake Rebecca Park Reserve
Picnicking, play area, mountain bike trails, boat rentals
Phone (763) 972-2620
Email see website
Web www.threeriversparkdistrict.org

Wayzata
Trolley Rides
Free trolley departs from the historic Wayzata Depot and circulates throughout the commercial district from mid-May to mid-October, Wednesday evening concerts at the depot, June into August
Phone (952) 473-9595
Web www.wayzatachamber.com

SW Regional LRT Trails

Vital Information:

Trail Distance: North Trail 16 miles, South Trail 12 miles

Trail Surface: limestone

Access Points: North: Hopkins, Excelsior, Victoria. South: Hopkins, Edenvale Park, Miller Park, Lake Riley Park, Chaska

Fees and Passes: none

Trail Website: www.threeriversparkdistrict.org

ABOUT THE TRAIL

These two former rail beds may someday become light rail corridors for the western suburbs. Until then, they supply bicycle escape routes to the western edges of the sprawling Twin Cities. The northern route is the older trail. It passes through the old wealth of Lake Minnetonka on its way to Carver Park Reserve. Marinas, mansions and money give way to a mix of rural land and suburban sprawl until the trail ends at the little town of Victoria. Carver Park Reserve is readily accessible from Victoria and worth the visit. The southern trail extends east toward Minneapolis. To the west it passes through a blend of new wealth and middle class subdivisions with a mix of lakes, parks and restored prairie.

TRAIL HIGHLIGHTS

Both trails begin in Hopkins, a suburb that has maintained a very comfortable, human-scale downtown. Stop in historic Excelsior for a stroll down Main Street, then take a shaded break at Excelsior Commons on the shore of Lake Minnetonka. Minnetonka has its own system of bike trails. The most interesting begins behind the Minnetonka High School and runs down to Purgatory Park, a 6 mile round trip including the trail through Purgatory Park. See trail map for details. The southern LRT trail skirts Shady Oak Lake and Lake Riley, then opens to a grand view of the Minnesota River and the Minnesota Valley Wildlife Refuge. From here to the southern trailhead at Bluff Creek Drive, the trail drops quickly.

ABOUT THE ROADS

Expect traffic on the roads in this area. The three main routes shown here connect the two trails together to create several loop options. For more information about road and trail routes in this area, pick up a copy of the Twin Cities Bike Map by Little Transport Press.

ROAD HIGHLIGHTS

Smithtown Road offers a quiet alternate to the trail. Low rolling hills and large estates dot this short stretch of road. Highways 43 and 10 still hold their rural charm and connect the two trails as they pass through rolling hills and open farm land.

HOW TO GET THERE

Hopkins is just off Highway 169 west of Minneapolis. Take Excelsior Boulevard (Highway 3) west about half a mile to 8th Ave. S. The southern trail begins at the back of the park-and-ride lot on the south side of Excelsior Blvd. You can park here for the north trail as well and take 8th Ave. to half a block north of Main Street. The trail begins behind a row of bushes. See city map for details. See the trail map for highway routes to other access points along the north and south trails.

Duluth

Hopkins Minneapolis
Victoria St. Paul
Chanhassen Red Wing
Winona

Rochester

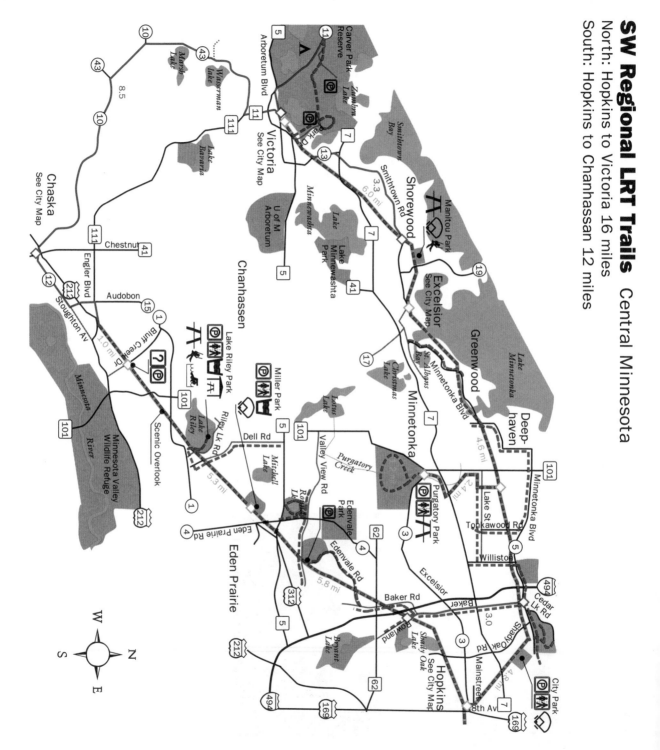

Hopkins

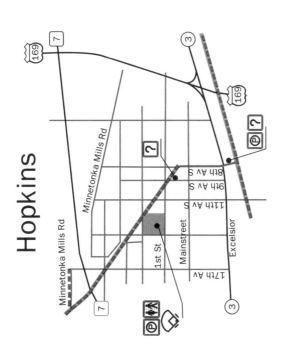

Chaska

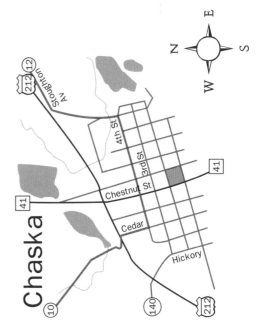

Excelsior

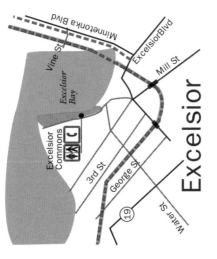

Victoria

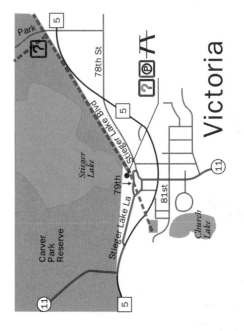

N
W   E
S

SW Regional LRT Trails Central Minnesota

TOURIST INFORMATION

Chaska Chamber of Commerce
Phone (952) 448-5000
Fax (952) 448-4261
Email chaska@chaska-chamber.org
Web www.chaska-chamber.org

Eden Prairie Chamber of Commerce
Phone (952) 944-2830
Fax (952) 944-0229
Email adminj@epchamber.org
Web www.epchamber.org

Eden Prairie City Hall
Phone (952) 949-8300
Fax (952) 949-8450
Web www.edenprairie.org

Excelsior Area Chamber of Commerce
Phone (952) 474-6461
Fax (952) 474-3139
Email eacc@isd.net
Web www.excelsiorchamber.com

Twin West Chamber of Commerce
Phone (952) 540-0234
Fax (952) 540-0237
Email info@twinwest.com
Web www.twinwest.com

LODGING

Motels/Resorts

Chanhassen
Country Suites by Carlson
591 West 78th Street
Phone (952) 937-2424

Hopkins
The Hopkins House
1501 Hwy 7
Phone (952) 935-7711
Fax (952) 943-5666

Camping

Victoria
Carver Park Reserve
7200 Victoria Drive

Phone (763) 559-6700
Email see website
Web www.threeriversparkdistrict.org

GROCERIES

Hopkins
Driskill's SuperValu
(952) 938-6301

BIKE RENTAL

Chaska
Get Your Gear Outfitters
Phone (952) 448-9911

BIKE REPAIR

Chanhassen
Bokoo Bikes
Phone (952) 934-6468
Email info@bokoobikes.com
Web www.bokoobikes.com

Chaska
Get Your Gear Outfitters
Phone (952) 448-9911
Fax (952) 448-7383

Eden Prairie
Chanhassen Bike and Ski
Phone (952) 942-8685

FESTIVALS AND EVENTS

St. Louis Park
Bikemasters
Phone (952) 848-0481

Hoigaards, Inc
Phone (952) 929-1351

Chaska

June
Taste of Chaska
Wednesday evening sometime in June,
call chamber for date
Phone (952) 448-5000
Web www.chaska-chamber.org

July
River City Days
Music, arts and crafts show, kids'
games, food booths, City Square Park,
Fourth Weekend
Phone (952) 448-5000
Web www.chaska-chamber.org

Eden Prairie

June
Lions Club Schooner Days Festival
Round Lake Park, family activities, car-
nival rides, softball tourney, first week-
end in June or last weekend in May
Phone (952) 934-7070
Web www.eplions.org

Central Minnesota **SW Regional LRT Trails**

FESTIVALS AND EVENTS cont'd

MN Festival of Jazz on the Prairie
Staring Lake Amphitheater, usually
second Sunday
Phone (952) 949-8450

July

4th of July celebration
Round Lake and Staring Lake Parks,
triathlon, softball tourney, mixed doubles tennis
Phone (952) 949-8450
Web www.edenprairie.org

August

Eden Prairie Lions Club corn feed
Round Lake Park, First Saturday
Phone (952) 934-7070
Web http://www.eplions.org

September

SunBonnet Day
Cummins Grill Homestead, old fashioned ice-cream social, usually second
weekend
Phone (952) 949-8450
Web www.edenprairie.org

Excelsior

May

Excelsior Boat Show
Boat displays in Lyman Park, food vendors, Excelsior streetcar rides, Third
Weekend
Phone (952) 474-6461
Web www.excelsiorchamber.com

Memorial Day Parade
Patriotic program and parade
Phone (952) 474-6461
Web www.excelsiorchamber.com

June

Art on the Lake
200 juried artists from all over the
U.S., food, music, kids' activities, at
Commons Park on Lake Minnetonka,

Second Weekend
Phone (763) 474-6461
Web www.excelsiorchamber.com

July

Fireman's Dance
Annual Friday night street dance sponsored by Excelsior Volunteer Fire Dept,
See website for date.
Phone (952) 474-6461
Web www.excelsiorchamber.com

Old Fashioned Fourth of July
Kids' parade, kids' fishing contest,
sand castle contest, 10k fun run, food
and entertainment, evening performance by Minnesota Orchestra, fireworks off Excelsior Bay
Phone (952) 474-6461
Web www.excelsiorchamber.com

September

Apple Day
Apples, antiques, art, accessories,
autumn harvest, entertainment, family
fun, Third Saturday
Phone (952) 474-6461
Web www.excelsiorchamber.com

Hopkins

July

Raspberry Festival
10 day celebration including golf tourney, Grand Day Parade, kids' fishing
contest, music in the park, softball,
volleyball, bike race, tent dances, 5-
mile run, Second Weekend
Phone (952) 931-0878
Web
www.hopkinsraspberryfestival.com

ALTERNATE ACTIVITIES

Chanhassen

Minnesota Landscape Arboretum
Over a thousand acres of rolling hills, grand vistas, display gardens, and plant collections, three mile drive/bike, hiking trails, picnic facilities, restaurant
Phone (952) 443-1400
Fax (952) 443-2521
Email bonnie@arboretum.umn.edu
Web www.arboretum.umn.edu

Eden Prairie

Summer Concert Series
Staring Lake Amphitheater, 7:00pm Sun, Wed, and Fri evenings mid-June through mid August
Phone (952) 949-8450
Web www.edenprairie.org

Eden Prairie Summer Theater
Staring Lake Amphitheater, middle to end of June, check web site for details.
Phone (952) 949-8450
Web www.edenprairie.org

Excelsior

Water Street shops
Antique and specialty shops, restaurants, Minnesota Transportation Museum, old train depot
Phone (952) 474-6461
Email eacc@isd.net
Web www.excelsiorchamber.com

Minnetrista

Lake Minnetonka Regional Park
Swimming, play area, boat launch
Phone (952) 474-4822
Email see website
Web www.threeriversparkdistrict.org

Victoria

Boorsma Farm
Farmer's market, pick your own strawberries and raspberries
Phone (952) 443-2068

Carver Park Reserve
3300 acres of marsh, tamarack swamp, rolling hills, wooded areas, lots of lakes, camping, hiking, biking, in-line skating, fishing, bird watching, picnic areas, fishing pier, boat launch, access to LRT Trail
Phone (763) 559-9000
Email see website
Web www.threeriversparkdistrict.org

Grimm Farm
Located in Carver Park, historic farm house under construction as an interpretive center
Phone (763) 559-9000
Email see website
Web www.threeriversparkdistrict.org

Lowry Nature Center
Located within Carver Park Reserve, hiking trails, free Sunday afternoon family programing, "Habitat" educational play area
Phone (763) 694-7650
Email see website
Web www.threeriversparkdistrict.org

Gateway Trail

Vital Information:

Trail Distance: 17 miles

Trail Surface: asphalt

Access Points: Cayuga St. (St. Paul, no parking), Arlington Ave., Phalen-Kellor Park, Flicek Park (Maplewood), Hadley Ave., numerous streets, Pine Point Park

Fees and Passes: none

Trail Website:
http://www.gatewaytrailmn.org

Part of the Willard Munger Trail, which will eventually run from St. Paul to Duluth, the Gateway provides an urban escape route from near downtown St. Paul to the countryside at Pine Point Park. The trail is very popular, for good reasons, and heavily used by bicyclists, in-line skaters and walkers, especially on weekends and holidays.

TRAIL HIGHLIGHTS

The western end, in St. Paul, passes golf courses, parks, cemeteries and other green spaces. Spur trails circle through Phalen Park near Keller and Phalen Lakes. The central portion runs along Highway 36 and is not attractive, but it does offer ice cream and fast food stops near the trail. North of Highway 36, the trail moves into a semi-rural area with lakes, fields and trees. Quite attractive, especially so close to an urban center. The trailhead at Pine Point has bathrooms, running water and some shade.

ABOUT THE ROADS

Flat to low rolling, the roads toward the northeastern end of the trail pass mostly through farm fields and wide open spaces. Traffic is generally low, but can spike occasionally or change because of new developments in the ex-urban lands around the city. For more road information, refer to the Twin Cities Bike Map by Little Transport Press.

ROAD HIGHLIGHTS

Take an out-and-back loop to Square Lake Park, about four and a half miles northeast of the Pine Point trailhead. The lake is pretty, clear and usually quiet. The park has a public beach and bathhouse. Withrow is a quiet little town just beyond the relentless urban sprawl. Traffic on Highways 9 and 66 will vary with the time of day and day of the week. The Demontreville Loop circles and passes between lakes, trees and housing developments. The little spur between Lakes Demontreville and Olson is at water's edge and passes through an older development with mature trees and narrow roads.

HOW TO GET THERE

See city and trail maps for details.

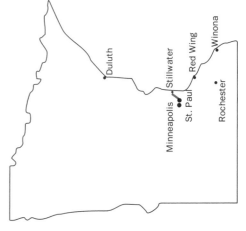

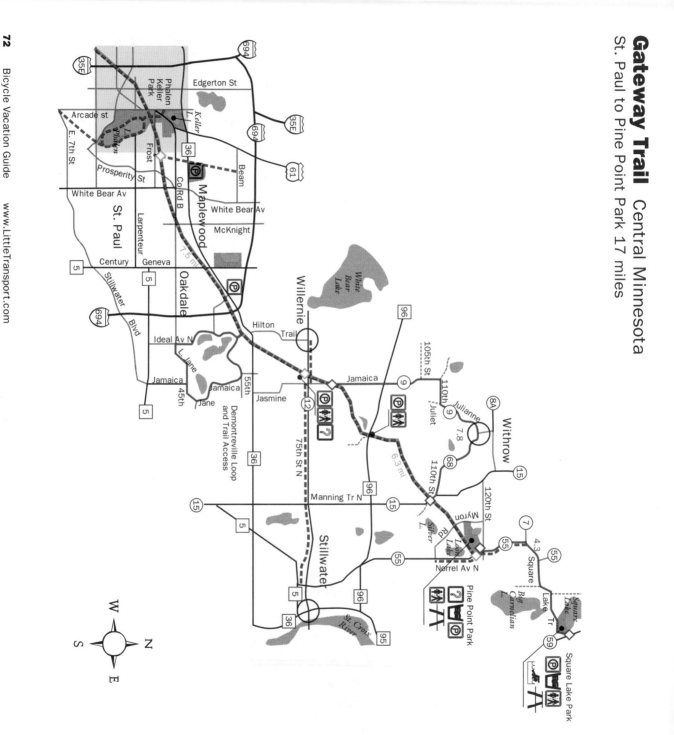

DNR
Toll Free (888) 646-6367
Phone (651) 296-6157
Fax (651) 297-3618
Email info@dnr.state.mn.us
Web www.dnr.state.mn.us

Greater Stillwater Chamber of Commerce
Phone (651) 439-4001
Fax (651) 439-4035
Email info@ilovestillwater.com
Web www.ilovestillwater.com

St. Paul Convention and Visitors Bureau
Toll Free (800) 627-6101
Phone (651) 265-4900
Fax (651) 265-4999
Email spcvb@stpaulcvb.org
Web www.stpaulcvb.org

The Gateway Trail Association
Email info@gatewaytrailmn.org
Web www.gatewaytrailmn.org

LODGING

Bed and Breakfast
Stillwater
Aurora Staples Inn
303 North Fourth Street
Phone (651) 351-1187
Web www.aurorastaplesinn.com

Lady Goodwood Bed & Breakfast
704 South First Street
Phone (651) 439-3771
Web www.ladygoodwood.com

The Ann Beane Mansion
319 W. Pine St.
Phone (651) 430-0355
Web www.annbeanmansion.com

The Elephant Walk
801 W. Pine St
Toll Free (888) 430-0359

Phone (651) 430-0359
Fax (651) 351-9080
Email info@elephantwalkbb.com
Web www.elephantwalkbb.com

The James A. Mulvey Inn
622 West Churchill Street
Phone (651) 430-8008
Web www.jamesmulveyinn.com

The Laurel St Inn
210 E. Laurel St.
Phone (651) 351-0031
Web www.laurelstreetinn.com

The Rivertown Inn
306 West Olive Street
Phone (651) 430-2955
Fax (651) 430-2206
Web www.rivertowninn.com

The William Sauntry Mansion
626 N. 4th St.
Phone (651) 430-2653
Web www.sauntrymansion.com

Camping
Hastings
Afton State Park
6959 Keller Ave. S
Phone (651) 436-5391
Web www.dnr.state.mn.us

Marine on the St.Croix
William O'Brien State Park
16821 O'Brien Trail N
Phone (651) 433-0500
Web www.dnr.state.mn.us

Stillwater
Len's Family Foods

Maplewood
Strauss Skates and Bicycles
Toll Free (888) 770-1344
Phone (651) 770-1344

St. Paul
Jacks Bike Shop
Phone (651) 488-9078

Stillwater
JA's Bikes
Phone (651) 275-0280
St. Croix Bike and Skate
Phone (651) 439-2337
Fax (651) 351-5434

St. Paul
May
Cinco de Mayo Mexican Fiesta
Parade, food and entertainment, West side of St. Paul, First Weekend
Toll Free (800) 627-6101
Phone (651) 222-6347
Web www.districtdelsol.com

Gateway Trail Central Minnesota

June

Festival of Nations
Multicultural celebration at RiverCentre, Check website for dates.
Toll Free (800) 627-6101
Phone (651) 265-4900
Web www.festivalofnations.com

Grand Old Day
Parade, entertainment, crafts, food and activities along Grand Ave, First Weekend
Toll Free (800) 627-6101
Phone (651) 699-0029
Web www.grandave.com

July

A Taste of Minnesota
4th of July celebration at the State Capitol grounds with music, food, and fireworks, Check web site for all dates.
Toll Free (800) 627-6101
Phone (651) 772-9980
Web www.tasteofmn.org

August

Irish Fair of Minnesota
Irish music, dancing, food and crafts, on Harriet Island. Second Weekend
Toll Free (800) 627-6101
Phone (952) 474-7411
Web www.irishfair.com

Minnesota State Fair
One of the largest state fairs in the U.S., Fourth Weekend
Toll Free (800) 627-6101
Phone (651) 642-2200
Web www.mnstatefair.org

May

Rivertown Art Fair
Arts, crafts, food, entertainment, in Lowell Park, Check web site for dates.
Phone (651) 439-4001

Web www.ilovestillwater.com

June

Music on the Waterfront
Free outdoor concerts at Lowell Park Wednesday evenings
Phone (651) 439-4001
Web info@ilovestillwater.com

July

Fourth of July
Parade and fireworks on the St. Croix
Phone (651) 439-4001
Web www.ilovestillwater.com

September

Lumberjack Days
Exhibitions, competitions, parade, 10k and half marathon runs, craft fair, food vendors, music, kids' games and rides, fireworks, Check web site for dates.
Phone (651) 439-4001
Web www.ilovestillwater.com

Oktoberfest
Polka bands and food, at Gasthaus Bavarian Hunter, Check website for dates.
Phone (651) 439-7128
Web www.gasthausbavarianhunter.com

October

Fall Colors Fine Art and Jazz Festival
Juried fine art, jazz bands and food ven-

dors, at Lowell Park, First Weekend
Phone (651) 439-4001
Web www.ilovestillwater.com

Marine on St. Croix

William O'Brien State Park
Camping, hiking, interpretive programs, canoe rental, swimming, picnicking
Toll Free (888) 646-6367
Phone (651) 433-0500
Web www.dnr.state.mn.us

Roseville

Harriet Alexander Nature Center
Trails through marsh, prairie and forest
Phone (651) 765-4262
Web www.ci.roseville.mn.us

St. Paul

Capitol City Trolley
Historical tours of downtown St. Paul, Thursdays, by reservation only
Phone (651) 223-5600
Fax (651) 793-8731

Como Park Zoo and Conservatory
Zoological exhibits, botanical gardens, summer concerts at Lakeside Pavilion
Phone (651) 487-8200
Web www.ci.stpaul.mn.us/depts/parks

Down In History Tours
Several tours, including the popular St. Paul Gangster Tour, haunts and hideouts of America's most notorious gangsters
Phone (651) 292-1220
Fax (651) 224-0059
Web www.wabashastreetcaves.com

Farmers Market
290 East 5th St. Saturday and Sunday mornings, May to November
Phone (651) 227-8101
Web www.stpaulfarmersmarket.com

Fitzgerald Theater
Home of Garrison Keillor's "A Prairie Home Companion" and other popular MPR shows. Check website for events.
Phone (651) 290-1221
Fax (651) 290-1195
Email fitzgerald@mpr.org
Web www.fitzgeraldtheater.org

Minnesota Children's Museum
Interactive children's museum geared to kids under 10 years old and their families
Phone (651) 225-6000
Email mcm@mcm.org
Web www.mcm.org

Minnesota Historical Society
Exhibits and demonstrations from Minnesota's past and present. Check website for events and tours at all society sites, state-wide.
Toll Free (800) 657-3773
Phone (651) 296-6126
Web www.mnhs.org

Minnesota Museum of American Art
Located in the impressive Landmark Center, diverse collection of American Art, including paintings, crafts and sculptures
Phone (651) 292-4355
Fax (651) 292-4340
Web www.mmaa.org

Minnesota State Capitol Tours
Tour the House, Senate, Supreme Court, and governor's reception room
Toll Free (800) 657-3773
Phone (651) 296-2881
Fax (651) 297-1502
Email statecapitol@mnhs.org
Web www.mnhs.org

Paddleford Packet Boat Company
Sternwheeler riverboat cruises on the Mississippi, from Harriet Island

Toll Free (800) 543-3908
Phone (651) 227-1100
Email info@riverrides.com
Web www.riverrides.com

Phalen Keller Park
Picnic areas, walking and bike trails, swimming, Wheelock Pky at Arcade St
Phone (651) 266-6400
Web www.ci.stpaul.mn.us/depts/parks

Science Museum of Minnesota
Hands-on science exhibits, world class collection of fossils and artifacts, Omnitheater
Toll Free (800) 221-9444
Phone (651) 221-9444
Fax (651) 221-4777
Email info@smm.org
Web www.smm.org

Stillwater

Aamodt's Apple Farm and St. Croix Vineyard
Pick your own or buy, hayrides, hot air balloon rides
Phone (651) 439-3127
Email see website
Web www.aamodtsapplefarm.com

Antique shopping
Minnesota's antique mecca, down-town area
Phone (651) 439-7700

Historic tours
Explore Stillwater, Minnesota's oldest town, by narrated trolley tours. Check website for details.
Phone (651) 430-0352
Fax (715) 549-6086
Email chamber@stllwtr.com
Web www.stillwatertrolley.com

Minnesota Zephyr
Elegant, restored dining train along the St. Croix River Valley with hits of the 40's and 50's by the Zephyr Cabaret
Toll Free (800) 992-6100
Phone (651) 430-3000
Email info@minnesotazephyr.com
Web www.minnesotazephyr.com

Nature's Nectar
Local honey, comb honey, beeswax products, and honey sticks for instant energy, Call ahead for hours.
Phone (651) 439-8793
Email naturesnectar@msn.com

Northern Vineyards
Downtown Stillwater, wine tasting, tours by appointment
Phone (651) 430-1032
Fax (651) 430-1331

Email northernvineyards@att.net
Web www.northernvineyards.com

Rockin' R Ranch
Carriage and hay rides, riding lessons, trail rides
Phone (651) 439-6878
Web www.ilovestillwater.com

Wolf Brewery Caves
10,000 square feet of caves, open for afternoon tours, Spring through Fall
Phone (651) 292-1220

Fax (651) 224-0059
Web www.wabashastreetcaves.com

White Bear Lake

Pine Tree Apple Orchards of White Bear Lake
Pick your own strawberries and apples, pumpkin patch, wagon rides, hiking in the orchards
Phone (651) 429-7202
Web www.pinetreeappleorchard.com

Cannon Valley Trail

Vital Information:

Trail Distance: 20 miles

Trail Surface: asphalt

Access Points: Cannon Falls, Welch Village, Red Wing

Fees and Passes: Wheel Pass $3.00/day, $12.00 perseason. No charge for children under 18.

Trail Website:
www.cannonvalleytrail.com

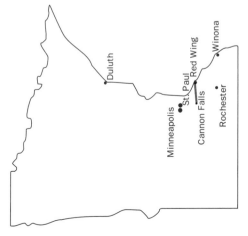

This former Chicago Great Western Rail Line runs along the south side of the Cannon River from Cannon Falls to Red Wing. Views from the trail include panoramic overlooks near Cannon Falls and intimate river bottom near Red Wing. The trail drops at a steady rate from Cannon Falls on the west to Red Wing on the east. Watch for old railway mileposts and a wide variety of wildflowers.

TRAIL HIGHLIGHTS

The bluffs come right up to the trail on the south and the river drops away to the north between Cannon Falls and Anderson Memorial Rest Area, creating spectacular panoramic views of the river and a damp micro environment supporting ferns, mosses and lichens. The city trail in Cannon Falls has scenic stretches. The city trail along Hay Creek in Red Wing is quite scenic and worth exploring.

ABOUT THE ROADS

This is bluff country. The marked routes are hilly, smooth, low traffic and rural in character. Ride all the way from end to end or cut back to the trail at the halfway point, near Welch Village. Roads to the north of the Cannon River tend to be gravel. Expect to climb from the trail to all road routes.

ROAD HIGHLIGHTS

County Road 1 climbs from the Mississippi River Valley in Red Wing to the rural highlands of Goodhue County. Once out of the river valley, expect

rolling ridge top to the town of White Rock, then more pronounced up and down to Highway 25. Traffic is heavy near Red Wing, so consider the alternate route laid out in the Red Wing City Map. Highway 25 climbs long and steady out of Cannon Falls, then settles into rolling ridge top to Highway 1. Highway 7 connects the trail to the tiny town of Vasa via a long climb, then rolls up and down to Highway 1. Check out the Vasa Museum and the nearby Lutheran Church on the hill. The cemetery next to the church has tombstones dating back to the middle 1800s. Baypoint Park, 1 mile west of the Red Wing Trailhead, has great facilities and a marina.

HOW TO GET THERE

Cannon Falls is off Hwy 52, about midway between the Twin Cities and Rochester. Red Wing is 45 miles southeast of St. Paul on Highway 61. To get to Welch Village, at the midpoint of the trail, take Hwy 7 south from Hwy 61, about 8 miles west of Red Wing. Watch for the Welch Village signs. See city maps for directions to trailheads in Cannon Falls and Red Wing.

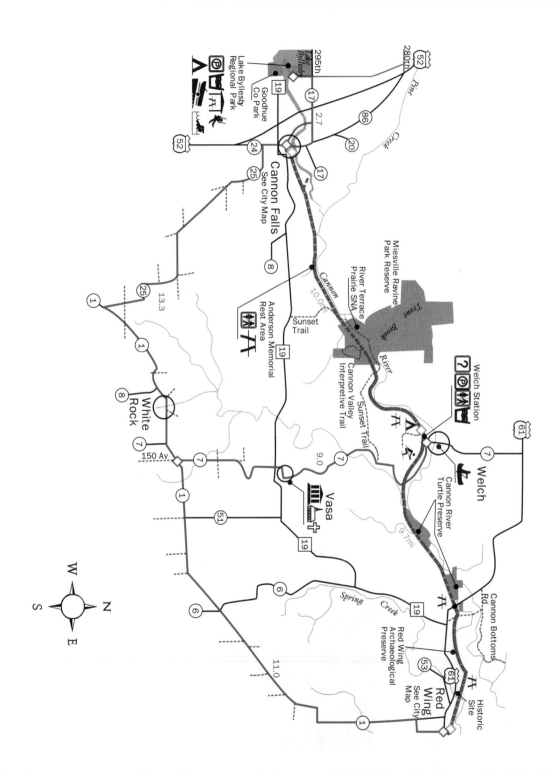

Lake Byllesby Regional Park
Goodhue Co Park
52
295th
Lake Byllesby
19
17
2.7
280th
52
86
20
24
25
Cannon Falls See City Map
8
Anderson Memorial Rest Area
19
Sunset Trail
Cannon
10.0mi
Pine Creek

Miesville Ravine Park Reserve
River Terrace Prairie SNA
Trout Brook
River
Sunset Trail
Cannon Valley Interpretive Trail
Welch Station
Welch
61
7
Cannon River Turtle Preserve
9.7mi

1
25
13.3
1
8
White Rock
7
150 Av
7
1
51
9.0
7
19
Vasa

6
6
Spring Creek
19
Cannon Bottoms Rd.
Red Wing Archaeological Preserve
53
61
Red Wing See City Map
Historic Site

11.0
1

N
W   E
S

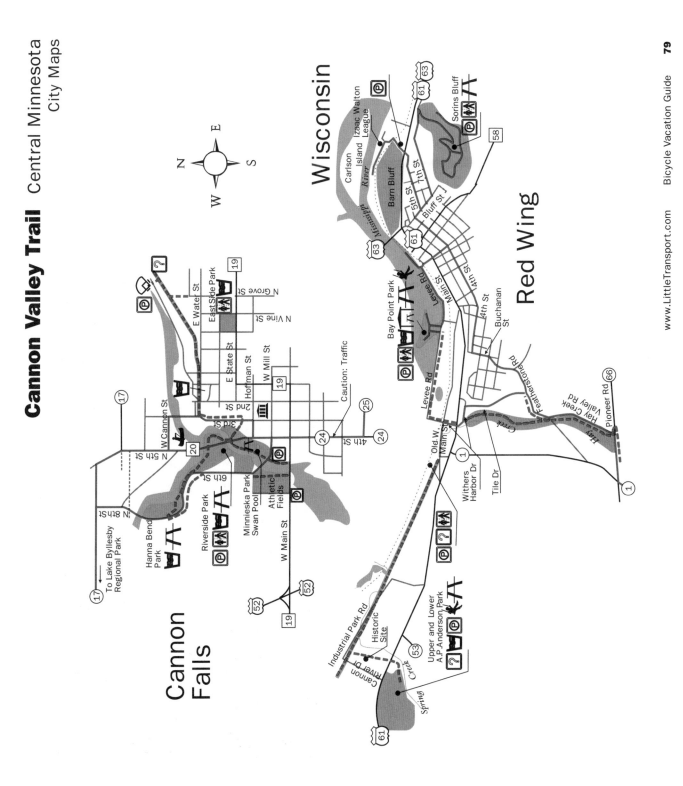

Cannon Valley Trail Central Minnesota
City Maps

Cannon Falls

Wisconsin

Red Wing

To Lake Byllesby Regional Park

Hanna Bend Park

Riverside Park

Minnieska Park Swan Pool

Athletic Fields

East Side Park

N Grove St
E Water St
N Vine St
E State St
Hoffman St
W Mill St
2nd St
3rd St
4th St
W Cannon St
N 5th St
6th St
N 8th St
W Main St

Caution: Traffic

Industrial Park Rd
Cannon River Dr
Historic Site
Spring Creek
Upper and Lower A.P. Anderson Park

Old W. Main St
Withers Harbor Dr
Tile Dr
Feathenstone Rd
Hwy
Creek
Hay Creek
Valley Rd
Pioneer Rd

Carlson Island
Izaac Walton League
Barn Bluff
Mississippi River
5th St
7th St
Bluff St
Bay Point Park
Levee Rd
Main St
14th St
4th St
Buchanan St

Sorins Bluff

Cannon Valley Trail Central Minnesota

Cannon Falls Chamber of Commerce
Phone (507) 263-2289
Fax (507) 263-2785
Email tourism@cannonfalls.org
Web www.cannonfalls.org

Cannon Valley Trail, Cannon Falls
Phone (507) 263-0508
Email info@cannonvalleytrail.com
Web www.cannonvalleytrail.com

Cannon Valley Trail, Welch
Phone (651) 258-4141

Red Wing Chamber of Commerce
Toll Free (800) 762-9516
Phone (651) 388-4719
Email chamber@redwingchamber.com
Web www.redwingchamber.com

Red Wing Visitor and Convention Bureau
Toll Free (800) 498-3444
Phone (651) 385-5934
Fax (651) 388-3900
Email info@redwing.org
Web www.redwing.org

Motels/Resorts

Cannon Falls

Caravan Motel
Highway 52
Phone (507) 263-4777

Red Wing

AmericInn
1819 Old West Main
Phone (651) 385-9060
Fax (651) 385-8139
Web www.americinnmn.net

Bed and Breakfast

Cannon Falls

Country Quiet Inn
37295 112th Ave. Way

Candlelight Inn
818 W. Third St
Toll Free (800) 254-9194
Phone (651) 388-8034
Email candlerw@rconnect.com
Web www.candlelightinn-redwing.com

The Golden Lantern Inn
721 East Ave
Toll Free (888) 288-3315
Phone (651) 388-3315
Email info@goldenlantern.com
Web www.goldenlantern.com

Quill and Quilt
615 West Hoffman St
Toll Free (800) 488-3849
Phone (507) 263-5507
Email info@quillandquilt.com
Web www.quillandquilt.com

Red Wing

Toll Free (800) 258-1843
Phone (651) 258-4406

Camping

Cannon Falls

Cannon Falls Campground
30365 Oak Lane
Phone (507) 263-3145
Web www.cannonfallscampground.com

Lake Byllesby Regional Park Campground
7650 Echo Point Rd
Phone (507) 263-4447

Frontenac

Frontenac State Park
Phone (651) 345-3401
Web www.dnr.mn.us

Lake City

Dorer Memorial Hardwood State Forest
1801 South Oak
Phone (651) 345-3216

LODGING cont'd

Red Wing
Hay Creek Valley Campground
31655 Hwy 58 Blvd
Toll Free (888) 388-3998
Phone (651) 388-3998

Welch
Hidden Valley Campground
27173 144 Avenue Way
Phone (651) 258-4550

GROCERIES

Cannon Falls
Cannon Econo Foods
(507) 263-3643

Red Wing
County Market
(651) 388-8258

BIKE RENTAL

Red Wing
Four Seasons Bike
Phone (651) 385-8614

The Route
Phone (651) 388-1082
Email adam@theroute.net
Web www.theroute.net

BIKE REPAIR

Red Wing
Four Seasons Bike
Phone (651) 385-8614

The Route
Phone (651) 388-1082
Email adam@theroute.net
Web www.theroute.net

FESTIVALS AND EVENTS

Cannon Falls
All Summer
Farmer's Market
Saturdays at downtown city parking
lot during growing season
Phone (507) 263-2289
Web www.cannonfalls.org

Voices of the Valley
Natural and cultural resource people
along the trail to answer questions on
a variety of topics, May through
September. First Saturday
Phone (507) 263-0508

May
Memorial Day Parade
Parade and service at Colvill Memorial
Phone (507) 263-2289
Web www.cannonfalls.org

July
Cannon Valley Fair
Parade, carnival, harness racing,
exhibits, fireworks, First Weekend
Phone (507) 263-2289
Web www.cannonfalls.org

Little Log House Antique Power
Antique and classic tractor show, flea
market, craft sale, home of the replica
of the famed Hastings Spiral Bridge,
Third Weekend
Phone (507) 263-2289
Web www.cannonfalls.org

August
Cruisin' Days
Friday night '50s car cruise and
dance, Saturday merchant Crazy Days,
Sunday Classic car show, First Sunday
Phone (507) 263-2289
Web www.cannonfalls.org

September
Community Wide Garage Sale
Third Saturday after Labor Day
Phone (507) 263-2289
Web www.cannonfalls.org

Red Wing
May
85 Mile Garage Sale
Residents and stores in the thirteen
river towns around Lake Pepin partici-
pate in a huge garage sale spectacular. First Weekend
Toll Free (888) 999-2619

Cannon Valley Trail Central Minnesota

July

Red Wing Collectors' Society
Red Wing Pottery Show with auctions,
sales, and seminars for adults and
children, Second Weekend
Toll Free (800) 977-7927
Phone (651) 385-5934

August

River City Days
Parade, family events, arts and crafts,
carnival, fireworks, at Bay Point Park,
First Weekend
Toll Free (800) 762-9516
Phone (651) 388-4719

October

Fall Festival of Arts
Juried art festival featuring 75 artists,
Minnesota book fair, film festival and
music, childrens' activities, food and
entertainment, downtown, Second
Weekend
Toll Free (800) 762-9516
Phone (651) 388-7569

Cannon Falls

Cannon Falls Historical Museum
Local history, call library for hours
Phone (507) 263-4080
Web www.cannonfalls.org

Countryside Antique Mall
Over 40 antique dealers under one roof
Phone (507) 263-0352
Web www.csantiques.com

Downtown Cannon Falls
29 downtown properties listed on the
National Registry of Historic Places
Phone (507) 263-2289
Fax (507) 263-2785
Email tourism@cannonfalls.org
Web www.cannonfalls.org

Frontenac

Frontenac State Park
Wooded bluffs with scenic views,
camping, boating, fishing, picnic
areas, Explore Old Frontenac — historic river town
Phone (651) 345-3401
Web www.dnr.state.mn.us

Red Wing

Antique shopping and architecture
walking tour
Downtown
Toll Free (800) 498-3444
Phone (651) 385-5934
Email info@redwing.org
Web www.redwing.org

Barn Bluff and Sorin's Bluff
Miles of bluff hiking above Red Wing
Phone (800) 498-3444
Email info@redwing.org
Web www.redwing.org

Goodhue County Historical Society
Kid-friendly historical museum: archae-
ology, early immigration and settlers,
local clay industry, rural school room,
Check website for details.
Phone (651) 388-6024
Email goodhuecountyhis@qwest.net
Web www.goodhuehistory.mus.mn.us

Historic Pottery District
Antique Alley, Redwing Pottery
salesroom, Pottery Place, factory out-
lets, specialty shops, eateries and
antique dealers, Old West Main St
Toll Free (800) 498-3444
Phone (651) 385-5934
Email info@rwpotteryplace.com
Web www.rwpotteryplace.com

Levee Park
Downtown on the Mississippi River,
docking site for Mississippi steam-
boats
Toll Free (800) 498-3444
Phone (651) 385-5934
Email info@redwing.org
Web www.redwing.org

Sheldon Theatre
Oldest municipally owned theater in
the US. Check website for events.
Toll Free (800) 899-5759
Phone (651) 385-3667
Web www.sheldontheatre.com

Sakatah Singing Hills Trail

Vital Information:

Trail Distance: 38 miles

Trail Surface: asphalt

Access Points: Fairbault, Warsaw, Morristown, Sakatah Lake State Park, Waterville, Elysian, Madison Lake, Mankato

Fees and Passes: none

Trail Website:
http://www.dnr.state.mn.us

ABOUT THE TRAIL

Running from a narrow, wooded valley called "Wardlaws Ravine" in Mankato through Sakatah Lake State Park and to the edge of Faribault, this trail passes through a number of attractive small towns and skirts large and small lakes. In-line skaters should be cautious at road and driveway crossings, they are often gravel. Trail towns offer parks, museums, and historic buildings.

TRAIL HIGHLIGHTS

The western section, from Mankato to Madison Lake, has the most diversity. It climbs through the heavily wooded, narrow valley of "Wardlaws Ravine", then opens up to wildflowers and farmland on the way to Madison Lake. The Elysian trail access is set in a pleasant little park with drinking water, modern bathrooms, and a sheltered picnic area. The trail stops at each edge of Waterville, but the road route connector is well marked and follows quiet residential streets. Pull off the trail at Sakatah State Park and head up to the lake for a pleasant break. Do the same a few miles further east at Morristown, where a short side trip will take you to the historic dam site and a quiet park along the Cannon River. The trail east of Morristown follows Highway 60 and loses some of its charm as a result.

ABOUT THE ROADS

The roads near the middle and eastern portions of the trail offer the best riding. They undulate over low to medium rollers past farm fields and woodlots, and skirt a number of mid-sized lakes. The routes on the trail map offer only a hint of the road riding options in this area. The roads near Mankato tend to have more, and faster moving, traffic.

ROAD HIGHLIGHTS

The wide range of cutting and milling tools in the steam powered Geldner Saw Mill are visible even when the museum is closed because of wide mesh steel grated doors. The mill is on the west edge of German Lake, northwest of Elysian. Highway 131 on the north edge of Sakatah Lake is a quiet, winding road with great views of Sakatah Lake State Park across the water. The roads north of the trail between Morristown and Faribault pass through gently rolling farmland and offer a great alternate to the trail.

HOW TO GET THERE

Take the Highway 60 exit off Interstate 35 at Faribault. The nearest trail access is at the Dairy Queen just west of the Interstate. See city map. All trail towns can be accessed from Highway 60 as you head west. The Mankato Trailhead is near the eastern edge of Mankato. Take the Highway 22 exit off Highway 14. Go north to Lime Valley Road. The trailhead is on the left, 0.2 miles north on Lime Valley Road.

Duluth
Minneapolis
St. Paul
Red Wing
Winona
Faribault
Mankato
Rochester

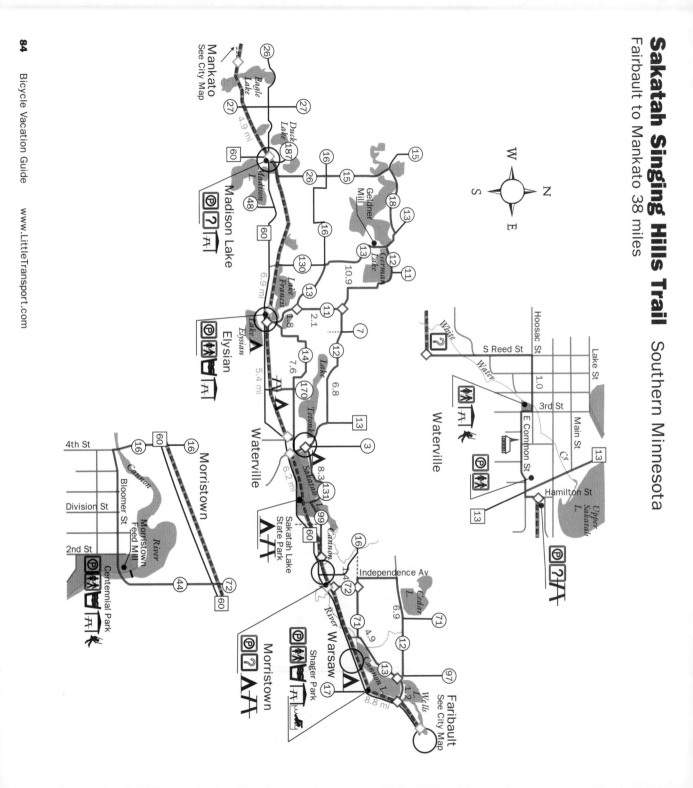

Sakatah Singing Hills Trail

Southern Minnesota

Fairbault to Mankato 38 miles

Southern Minnesota **Sakatah Singing Hills Trail**
City Maps

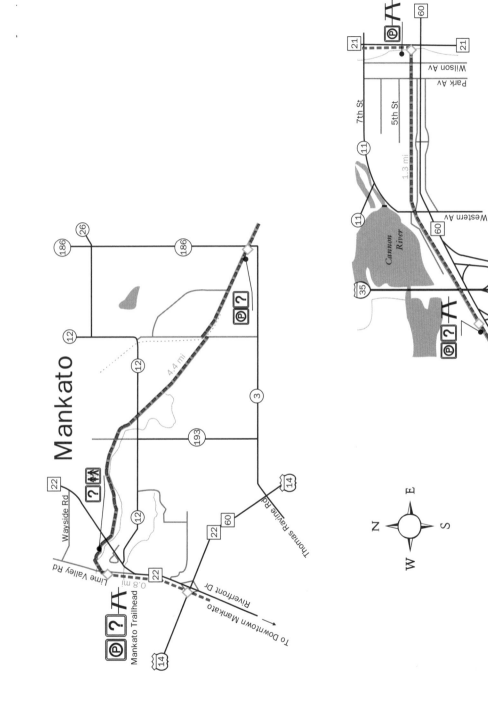

Mankato

Faribault

Sakatah Singing Hills Trail Southern Minnesota

Elysian Tourism Center
Toll Free (800) 507-7787
Phone (507) 267-4040
Fax (507) 267-4750
Email Use website form
Web www.elysianmn.com

Faribault Chamber of Commerce
Toll Free (800) 658-2354
Phone (507) 334-4381
Fax (507) 334-1003
Web www.faribaultmn.org

Mankato Area Convention and Visitors
Bureau
Toll Free (800) 657-4733
Phone (507) 345-4519
Fax (507) 345-4451
Email info@greatermankato.com
Web www.mankato.com

Morristown City Hall
Phone (507) 685-2302
Fax (507) 685-2632
Email motown@means.net
Web www.ci.morristown.mn.us

Sakatah Singing Hills State Trail Office
Toll Free (800) 507-7787
Phone (507) 267-4040
Web www.dnr.state.mn.us

Waterville Chamber of Commerce
Phone (507) 362-4609
Email lmesk@frontiernet.net
Web www.watervillemn.com

Motels/Resorts

Elysian
Lotus Lodge Motel
1/2 Way Point of Trail
511 W. Hwy 60
Phone (507) 267-4212

Faribault
AmericInn Motel & Suites
1801 Lavender Drive
Toll Free (800) 634-3444
Phone (507) 334-9464
Fax (507) 334-0616

Days Inn
1920 Cardinal Lane
Phone (507) 334-6835
Fax (507) 333-4636

Galaxie Inn & Suites
1401 Hwy 60 W
Toll Free (888) 334-9294
Phone (507) 334-5508
Email manwerk@yahoo.com
Web www.galaxieinnfaribault.com

Select Inn
4040 Hwy 60 W
Toll Free (800) 641-1000
Phone (507) 334-2051

The Lyndale Motel
904 Lyndale Ave N
Toll Free (800) 559-4386
Phone (507) 334-4386

Waterville
Lakeview Resort
14972 Sakatah Lake Rd
PO Box 164

Phone (507) 362-4616
Web www.mnlakeviewresort.com

Sakatah Bay Resort Motel
815 E. Paquin Street
Phone (507) 362-8980
Web www.sakatahbay.com

Camping

Elysian
Silver's Resort
North Shore Lake Elysian
PO Box 205
Phone (507) 267-4694

Faribault
Camp Faribo Campground/RV Park
21851 Bagley Ave
Toll Free (800) 689-8453
Phone (507) 332-8453

Waterville
Kamp Dels
North Shore Lake Sakatah
Phone (507) 362-8616
Web www.kampdels.com

Lakeview Resort
14972 Sakatah Lake Rd
PO Box 164
Phone (507) 362-4616
Web www.mnlakeviewresort.com

Sakatah Lake State Park Campground
50499 Sakatah Lake State Park Rd
Phone (507) 362-4438
Web www.dnr.state.mn.us

Southern Minnesota **Sakatah Singing Hills Trail**

GROCERIES

Elysian
D & B Foods
(507) 267-4447

Faribault
Faribault Foods
(507) 331-1400

Hy Vee Food Store
(507) 334-2085

BIKE RENTAL

Mankato
A-1 Bike Shop
Phone (507) 625-2453

Waterville
Ron's Hardware Hank
Phone (507) 362-4308

BIKE REPAIR

Faribault
The Village Pedaler
Phone (507) 331-2636

Mankato
A-1 Bike Shop
Phone (507) 625-2453

Keir's Wheelwright
Phone (507) 387-2728

Scheels Sport Shop
Phone (507) 386-7767
Fax (507) 386-7772
Web www.scheelssports.com

University Cycle
Phone (507) 340-7232

Waterville
Ron's Hardware Hank
Phone (507) 362-4308

mile bike, 4 mile run, Saturday after
the 4th
Phone (507) 267-4231
Web www.elysianmn.com

Faribault
All Summer
Farmers Market
Every Wednesday afternoon and
Saturday morning during growing sea-
son, at Central Park
Phone (507) 332-8283

June
Heritage Days and Rock Island Art
Festival
Celebrating the diverse heritage and
cultures that comprise Faribault,
parade, carnival, arts and crafts show,
kids' fishing contest, bike tour, tours
of historical buildings, Third Weekend
Toll Free (800) 658-2354
Phone (507) 334-4381
Web www.faribaultmn.orgFestivals

FESTIVALS AND EVENTS

Elysian
July
Fourth of July Festival
Parade, kids' fishing contest, milk jug
regatta, pageant, dance, flea market,
3 day event
Toll Free (800) 507-7787
Phone (507) 267-4040
Web www.elysianmn.com

Rookies' Triathlon
Seven age categories, .4 mile swim, 8

July

Rice County Free Fair

Food, derby races, coronation, rodeo, five day event at the fairgrounds, Third Weekend

Toll Free (800) 658-2354

Phone (507) 334-4381

Web www.faribaultmn.org

September

Balloon Air-a-Rama

Hot air balloon exhibition, antique aircraft display, glider demonstrations, airplane rides, food vendors, at Municipal Airport, Check website for dates.

Toll Free (800) 658-2354

Phone (507) 334-4381

Web www.faribaultmn.org

Minnesota State Rodeo

State rodeo championships, Labor Day

Toll Free (800) 658-2354

Phone (507) 334-4381

Web www.faribaultmn.org

Tree Frog Music Festival

Music, art, food, twenty diverse music acts, original art, childrens' activities, at Teepee Tonka Park, Check website for dates.

Toll Free (800) 658-2354

Phone (507) 334-4381

Web www.faribaultmn.org

October

Taste of Faribault

Sample food from local vendors at the American Legion, Third Thursday

Toll Free (800) 658-2354

Phone (507) 334-4381

Web www.faribaultmn.org

Madison Lake

July

Paddlefish Days

Parade, street dance, fun run, fire department open house, Fourth Weekend

Phone (507) 243-3011

Mankato

July

Mankato Vikings Training Camp

At Blakeslee Field, Minnesota State University Mankato, mid July through mid August

Toll Free (800) 657-4733

Phone (507) 345-4519

North Mankato Fun Days

Community celebration featuring food, parade, high school marching bands, horseshoe tournament, entertainment, Check website for dates.

Toll Free (800) 657-4733

Phone (507) 345-4519

Web www.nmpd.org

September

Mankato Mdewakanton Pow Wow

Native food, crafts, ceremonial dancing, and singing, Land of Memories Park, Second or Third Weekend

Toll Free (800) 657-4733

Phone (507) 345-4519

Web www.turtletrack.org/MahkatoWacipi

Morristown

June

Dam Days

Twilight parade Friday, carnival, family events, kids' parade, American Legion steak fry, First weekend after Memorial Day

Phone (507) 685-4155

Web www.ci.morristown.mn.us

Southern Minnesota **Sakatah Singing Hills Trail**

Waterville

June

Bullhead Days
Pageant, carnival, parade, food stands (including deep fried bullhead), 10k run and bike race, kids' fishing contest, Second weekend after Memorial Day
Phone (507) 362-4609
Web www.watervillemn.com

ALTERNATE ACTIVITIES

Elysian

Elysian City Park and Beach
Public swimming beach, sand volley-ball courts, picnic shelters
Phone (507) 267-4708
Web www.elysianmn.com

Klondike Hill
Highest point in three counties, one of the first Jesse James gang campsites
Phone (507) 267-4708
Web www.elysianmn.com

LeSueur County Historical Society
Displays and tours, open weekends.
Phone (507) 267-4620
Email lchsmuseum@frontiernet.net
Web www.frontiernet.net/~lchsmu-seum/

Okaman Cervidae Elk Farm
View a majestic herd of elk at restored historic farm.
Phone (507) 267-4054
Email okaman@frontiernet.net
Web www.okamanonline.com

Faribault

Faribault Art Center
Local artists on display, pottery and basket making, downtown Faribault
Phone (507) 332-7372
Web www.faribaultart.org

Faribault Woolen Mills
Tour the mill and shop the outlet store
Toll Free (800) 448-9665
Phone (507) 334-1644
Email store@faribowool.com
Web www.faribowool.com

Rice County Historical Society Museum
Varied exhibits, tours of Alexander Faribault House
Phone (507) 332-2121
Email rch@rchistory.org
Web www.rchistory.org

River Bend Nature Center
Forest, prairie, wetland, and riverbank, nine miles of marked trails, call for programs
Phone (507) 332-7151
Fax (507) 332-0656
Email rbncinfo@rbnc.org
Web www.rbnc.org

Mankato

Blue Earth County Historical Society
Varied exhibits at the Blue Earth County Heritage Center and at Hubbard House, a restored Victorian home
Phone (507) 345-5566
Email bechs@juno.com
Web www.rootsweb.com/~mnbechs

Highland Summer Theater
Four musicals and plays presented dur-ing the summer season at Minnesota State University, Call for brochure.
Phone (507) 389-6661
Web www.msutheatre.com

Minneopa State Park
Native prairie area, hiking and bird-watching, interpretive drive, explore the only major waterfall in southwest-ern Minnesota, old stone mill and van-ished village
Phone (507) 389-5464
Web www.dnr.state.mn.us

Waterville

Minnesota Fish Hatchery
Two miles west of Waterville on Cty 14, Call for tours.
Phone (507) 362-4223

Sakatah Lake State Park
Camping, picnicking, hiking, canoe and boat rentals, swimming, interpre-tive center
Phone (507) 362-4438
Web www.dnr.state.mn.us

Douglas Trail

Vital Information:

Trail Distance: 12 miles

Trail Surface: asphalt

Access Points: Pine Island, Douglas, Rochester

Fees and Passes: none

Trail Website: www.dnr.state.mn.us/state

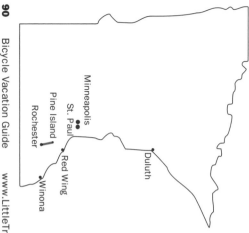

ABOUT THE TRAIL

This short, popular trail has two great access points, at Pine Island and Douglas, and a surprising number of amenities. The trail passes primarily through flat, rich agricultural land and ends on the north side of Rochester. The Mayo Clinic and most of the city's services are 10 miles from the trailhead.

TRAIL HIGHLIGHTS

Watch for irregular knobs of land protruding above the landscape about 3.5 miles south of Pine Island, followed by a slight rise into a wooded hillside. The trailhead in Douglas provides a pleasant, shaded rest stop.

ABOUT THE ROADS

Flat near the north and south ends of the trail, hilly and scenic just north of Douglas, these rural, lightly traveled roads cross the trail and pass near it, but offer an entirely different look at the land.

ROAD HIGHLIGHTS

Going north from Douglas, County Road 3 climbs for about a mile to a ridgetop with great overviews of the valley below. Then it's up and down for another half dozen miles until paying-back time with a long, swift, scenic descent into the flatlands. Finish by entering the south end of Pine Island. See city map for route through town to the trailhead.

HOW TO GET THERE

Pine Island is just off Hwy 52 about 70 miles south of the Twin Cities. Take the Hwy 11 exit. Trailhead is half a mile west of the highway. See city map. Rochester is 83 miles south of the Twin Cities on Hwy 52. Take the 14th St. NW/15th St. NW exit. Go west on 14th St. NW to Valleyhigh Drive. Turn right. Valleyhigh becomes Olmsted County Highway 4. Continue to trailhead. Distance from intersection of 14th and Valleyhigh Drive to trailhead is 2.1 miles. See city map.

Southern Minnesota **Douglas Trail**
Pine Island to Rochester 12 miles

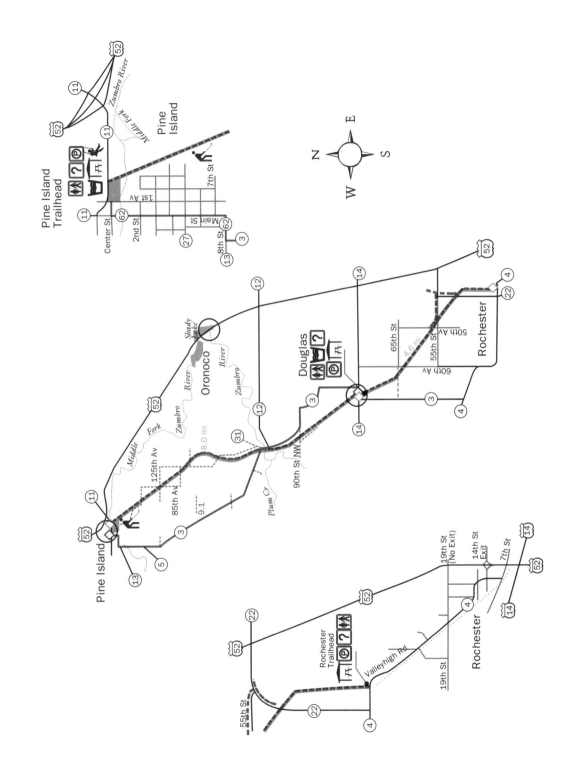

Douglas Trail Southern Minnesota

TOURIST INFORMATION

Rochester Convention and Visitors Bureau
Toll Free (800) 634-8277
Phone (507) 288-4331
Fax (507) 288-9144
Email info@rochestercvb.org
Web www.rochestercvb.org

LODGING

Motels/Resorts

Rochester

AmericInn Hotel & Suites
5708 Hwy 52 N.W.
Toll Free (800) 634-3444
Phone (507) 289-3344

Country Inn & Suites
4323 Hwy 52 N. & W. Frontage Rd
Toll Free (800) 456-4000
Phone (507) 285-3335

Camping

Pine Island

Wazionja Campground
6450 120th St NW
Phone (507) 356-8594

GROCERIES

Rochester

Good Food Store Co-op
(507) 289-9061

BIKE REPAIR

Rochester

Bicycle Sports, Inc.
Phone (507) 281-5007
Fax (507) 280-5878
Email gritman@bicyclesportsinc.com
Web www.bicyclesportsinc.com

Honest Bike Shop
Phone (507) 288-8888
Web www.honestbikeshop.com

Rochester Cycling and Fitness
Phone (507) 289-7410
Fax (507) 287-0563
Email info@cycling-fitness.com
Web www.cycling-fitness.com

FESTIVALS AND EVENTS

Rochester

All Summer

Down By The Riverside Concerts
Free evening concerts by various musical groups, mid-July through mid-August, Mayo Park, Call for schedule.
Toll Free (800) 634-8277
Phone (507) 288-4331
Web www.rochestercvb.org

May

Med City Marathon
Marathon and 2 & 4 person relay, Sunday before Memorial Day
Toll Free (800) 634-8277
Phone (507) 288-4331
Web www.medcitymarathon.com.

June

Mayowood Garden Tour and Flower Show
Tour the Mayowood Mansion and several private gardens, Last Saturday in June
Toll Free (800) 634-8277
Phone (507) 282-9447
Web www.olmstedhistory.com

Rochesterfest
Street dance, parade, live music, food vendors and family entertainment, Week long celebration, mid-June
Toll Free (800) 634-8277
Phone (507) 285-8769
Web www.rochestercvb.org

July

4th of July Celebration
Water Ski Club performs at Silver Lake, food vendors and fireworks, First Weekend
Toll Free (800) 634-8277
Phone (507) 288-4331
Web www.rochestercvb.org

Olmsted County Fair
Exhibits, food and entertainment at the fairgrounds, Check website for dates.
Toll Free (800) 634-8277
Phone (507) 282-0519
Web www.rochestercvb.org

August

Greek Festival
Music, food, and dance, call for info
Toll Free (800) 634-8277
Phone (507) 282-1529
Web www.rochestercvb.org

Southern Minnesota **Douglas Trail**

Threshing Show
Food, demos of early crafts and 19th century era threshing show, Olmsted County History Center, Check website for dates.
Toll Free (800) 634-8277
Phone (507) 282-9447
Web www.olmstedhistory.com.

September

Fall Harvest Fest
Nature related activities and crafts, canoeing, rock climbing wall, minnow races, live music, food wagon, Quarry Hill Nature Center
Phone (507) 281-6114
Web http://www.rschooltoday.com

Olmsted County Gold Rush Days
Antique show, flea market and food vendors at the fairgrounds, three times each year, Check website for dates.
Phone (507) 288-0320
Web www.iridescenthouse.com

Three Rivers Rendezvous
Participants dressed as early frontiersmen live in replica teepees and frontier tents, cook over open fires and demonstrate their mastery of early skills. Olmsted County History Center grounds. Fourth Weekend
Toll Free (800) 634-8277

Email grmunson@rochester.k12.mn.us
Web www.rschooltoday.com

Rochester Art Center
Fine arts and crafts, ongoing exhibits, free admission
Phone (507) 282-8629
Fax (507) 282-7737
Email see website
Web www.rochesterusa.com/artcenter

Sekapp Orchard
Pick your own strawberries and raspberries
Phone (507) 282-4544
Web www.mnfarmtours.com/sekapp.html

Silver Lake Park
Biking, rollerblading, jogging, paddleboat and canoe rentals, picnicking, children's adventure playground, outdoor pool
Phone (507) 281-6160
Fax (507) 281-6165
Web www.ci.rochester.mn.us/park

Phone (507) 282-9447
Web www.olmstedhistory.com.

ALTERNATE ACTIVITIES

Rochester

Mayo Clinic Tours
Behind the scenes walking tour, learn about Mayo's origins, art and architecture. Mondays through Fridays at 10 am
Phone (507) 538-0440
Email info@mayo.edu
Web www.mayoclinic.com

Olmsted County History Center & Museum
Pictures, maps, diaries, exhibits, restored pioneer log cabin and one-room schoolhouse
Phone (507) 282-9447
Email ochs@olmstedhistory.com
Web www.olmstedhistory.com

Quarry Hill Nature Center
Hiking trails, bike trail that connects to town, interactive displays and exhibits, 1700 gallon aquarium, live bee display, life-size model T-Rex head
Phone (507) 281-6114
Fax (507) 287-1345

Root River Trail

Vital Information:

Trail Distance: 43 miles

Trail Surface: asphalt

Access Points: Fountain, Lanesboro, Whalan, Peterson, Rushford, Houston

Fees and Passes: none

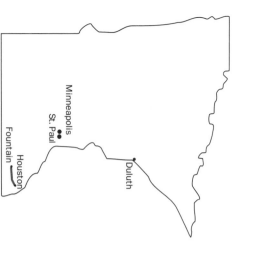

ABOUT THE TRAIL

A former Milwaukee Road railbed running through the blufflands and Amish country of southeast Minnesota, the trail follows and crosses the Root River as it passes beneath towering bluffs. The scenery is exceptional and the wildlife abundant. Expect to see hawks and vultures riding wind currents near the bluffs, wild turkeys in the woods, and deer in the open fields. Lanesboro, with its entire Main Street designated a historic district, is the best known town on the trail, but Rushford offers a unique museum in its two story depot, Whalan is known for its pies and the Houston Trailhead is a combination Nature Center, restroom and showers.

TRAIL HIGHLIGHTS

Check out the Karst landscape near Fountain. Karst is a type of topography characterized by sinkholes, caves and underground channels. The Harmony - Preston Valley Trail begins just east of the Isinours Unit. See Harmony–Preston Valley Trail for details. The dam and road cut on the western edge of Lanesboro create a dramatic first impression of the trail if you start from Lanesboro and ride west. East of Lanesboro, the trail hugs the Root River for some miles as it squeezes between the bluffs and the river. For a change of pace, start and end your trip in Houston. The trail is very scenic and underused between Rushford and Houston.

ABOUT THE ROADS

From the Valley of the Root River to the top of the bluffs, the roads will lead you through all the terrain that you only see from the trail. The options are endless, sometimes the hills will feel the same. Low traffic, generally good asphalt, watch for Amish vehicles, buffalo farms and 40 mile per hour descents off the bluffs. Expect to climb in any direction as you go away from the Root River.

ROAD HIGHLIGHTS

Highway 13 from Houston climbs steeply through a couple of 10 mph switchbacks to the ridgetop. Highway 30 is quite flat from Arendahl to several miles east of Highway 25, then begins a rapid descent towards Rushford. The first few miles of the descent pass through a narrow, intimate valley. Highways 21 and 10, south of the trail, have been re-paved recently. The climb from Lanesboro to Highway 12 is long and fairly steep. Watch for the buffalo farm at the intersection of Highways 10 and 12.

HOW TO GET THERE

Fountain, the western terminus, is about 30 miles south of Rochester on Highway 52. Continue on Highway 52 to Highway 16 for access to Lanesboro and other towns along the trail. From the east, take Interstate 90 west from LeCrescent about 25 miles to Highway 16. Rushford is about 10 miles south of Interstate 90 on Highway 16. See trail and city maps for details.

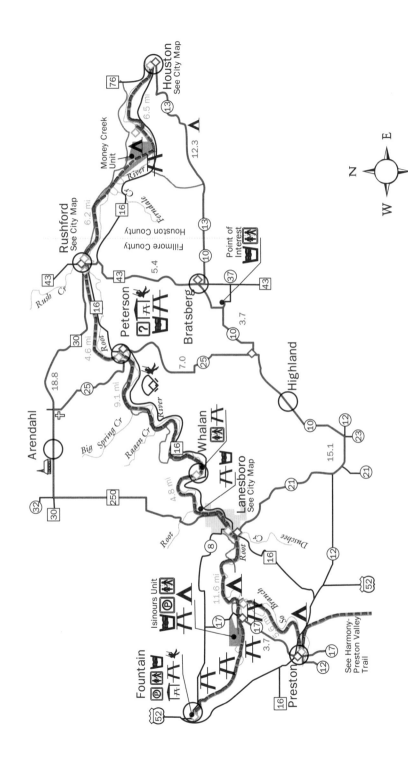

Southern Minnesota **Root River Trail**
Fountain to Houston 43 miles

Houston
See City Map

Money Creek Unit

Rushford
See City Map

Fillmore County
Houston County

Point of Interest

Peterson

Bratsberg

Highland

Arendahl

Whalan

Lanesboro
See City Map

Isinours Unit

Fountain

Preston

See Harmony-Preston Valley Trail

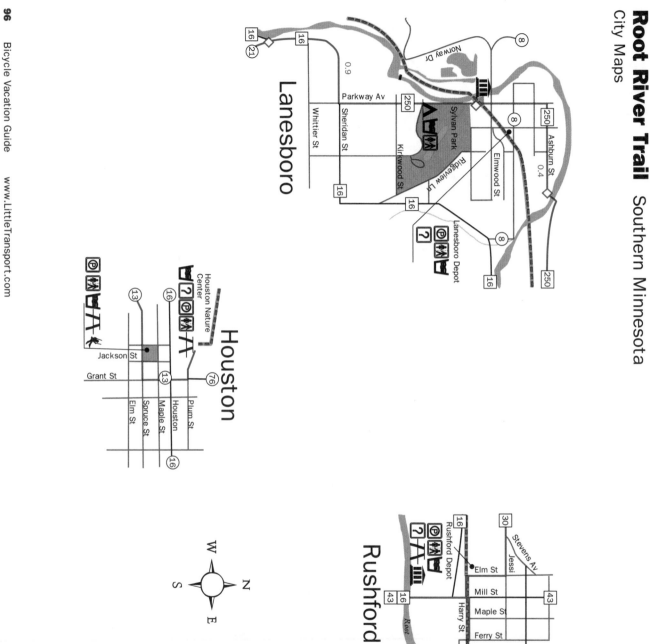

Lanesboro

Houston

Rushford

TOURIST INFORMATION

City of Fountain
Phone (507) 268-4923
Web www.bluffcountry.com

Historic Bluff Country Convention &
Visitors Bureau
Toll Free (800) 428-2030
Phone (507) 886-2230
Email hbc@means.net
Web www.bluffcountry.com

Houston Nature Center
Phone (507) 896-4668
Email nature@acegroup.cc
Web www.houstonmn.com

Lanesboro Chamber of Commerce
Toll Free (800) 944-2670
Phone (507) 467-2696
Email LVC@acegroup.cc
Web www.lanesboro.com

Rushford Area Chamber of Commerce
Phone (507) 864-3338
Email info@rushfordmn.com
Web www.rushfordmn.com

LODGING

Motels/Resorts

Lanesboro

Brewster's Red Hotel
Phone (507) 467-2999

Green Gables Inn
303 W. Sheridan

Toll Free (800) 818-4225
Phone (507) 467-2936
Email green@acegroup.cc
Web www.686.us/greengablesinn

Peterson

Geneva's Hideaway
87 Centennial St.
Toll Free (877) 727-4816
Phone (507) 875-7733
Web www.genevashideaway.com

Wenneson Historic Inn
425 Prospect St.
PO Box 11
Phone (507) 875-2587
Web www.wennesonhistoricinn.com

Bed and Breakfast

Houston

Addie's Attic B&B
117 South Jackson Street, PO Box 677
Phone (507) 896-3010
Web www.bluffcountry.com

The Bunkhouse
501 S. Jefferson
Phone (507) 896-2080
Web www.bluffcountry.com

Lanesboro

Berwood Hill Inn
Toll Free (800) 803-6748
Phone (507) 765-2391
Web www.berwood.com

Cady Hays House
500 Calhoun Ave
Phone (507) 467-2621
Email cadyhbb@acegroup.cc

Cozy Quilt Cottage
RR2-Box 9
Phone (507) 467-2458
Email weaveab@acegroup.cc

Habberstad House Bed and Breakfast
706 Fillmore Ave. S
Phone (507) 467-3560
Fax (507) 467-3472
Email habrstad@acegroup.cc
Web www.habberstadhouse.com

Hillcrest Hide-away B&B
404 Hillcrest St
Phone (507) 467-3079
Email hillcresthideaway@yahoo.com
Web www.hillcresthideaway.com

Historic Scanlon House
708 Parkway Ave. S
Toll Free (800) 944-2158
Phone (507) 467-2158
Web www.scanlonhouse.com

Mrs. B's Inn & Restaurant
101 Parkway Ave. N
Toll Free (800) 657-4710
Phone (507) 467-2154

Rushford

Meadows Inn B&B
900 Pine Meadows Lane
Phone (507) 864-2378
Fax (507) 864-3378
Web www.meadowsinn.com

River Trail Inn
202 South Mill Street
Toll Free (800) 584-6764
Phone (507) 864-7886

Sweet Dreams B&B
RR1, Box 19
Phone (507) 864-2462

Camping

Houston

Cushon's Peak Campground
18696 Hwy 16
Phone (507) 896-7325
Email camppeak@acegroup.cc
Web www.acegroup.cc

LODGING cont'd

Lanesboro
Eagle Cliff Campground & Lodging
3 miles east of Lanesboro on Hwy 16,
RR1, PO Box 344
Phone (507) 467-2598
Web www.eaglecliff-campground.com

Sylvan Park/Riverview Campground
City Park in Lanesboro
Phone (507) 467-3722

Peterson
Peterson RV Campground
Phone (507) 875-2587

Preston
The Old Barn Resort
Rt 3, Box 57
Toll Free (800) 552-2512
Phone (507) 467-2512
Web www.exploreminnesota.com

Rushford
North End Park
City Park in Rushford
Phone (507) 864-7949

GROCERIES

Fountain
Willie's Grocery & Locker
(507) 268-4488

Rushford
Rushford IGA
Phone (507) 864-2878

BIKE RENTAL

Lanesboro
Eagle Cliff Campground
Phone (507) 467-2598
Web www.eaglecliff-campground.com

Little River General Store
Toll Free (800) 994-2943
Phone (507) 467-2943
Email lrgenstore@aol.com

Web www.lrgeneralstore.com
Root River Outfitters
Phone (507) 467-3400
Email rro@acegroup.cc
Web www.rootriveroutfitters.com

Rushford
Geneva's Hideaway
Toll Free (877) 727-4816
Phone (507) 875-7733
Email genevas@acegroup.cc
Web www.genevashideaway.com

BIKE REPAIR

Lanesboro
Little River General Store
Toll Free (800) 994-2943
Phone (507) 467-2943
Email lrgenstore@aol.com
Web www.lrgeneralstore.com

FESTIVALS AND EVENTS

Houston

May
Bluff Country Bird Festival
Eagle Bluff Environmental Learning
Center. Check website for details.
Toll Free (800) 428-2030
Phone (507) 886-2230
Web www.bluffcountry.com

July
Bluegrass Festival
Money Creek Haven Campground. Last
Weekend
Phone (507) 896-3544
Web www.moneycreekhaven.com

Hoedown Days
Flea market, quilt display, antique car
and tractor, soap box derby, live
music, parade. Last full weekend
Phone (507) 896-3010
Web www.houstonmn.com

Lanesboro

June
Art in the Park
Artisans and crafters, childrens' activi-
ties, photo contest, Father's Day
Toll Free (800) 944-2670
Phone (507) 467-2696
Web www.lanesboro.com

August
Buffalo Bill Days
Parade, flea market, brat and beer gar-
den, live theater, volleyball and soft-
ball tourneys, First Weekend
Toll Free (800) 944-2670
Phone (507) 467-2696
Web www.lanesboro.com

October
Fall Fest
German Polkafest, First Saturday
Toll Free (800) 944-2670
Phone (507) 467-2696
Web www.lanesboro.com

Peterson

June
Gammel Dag Fest
City-wide celebration, Third Weekend
Phone (507) 875-2247

Rushford

July
Rushford Days
Parade, crafts, antiques, volleyball and
softball tourneys, Third Weekend
Phone (507) 864-2444
Web www.rushfordmn.com

Eagle Bluff Environmental Learning Center
Hiking trails, bat condominium, raptor viewing from the bluffs, treetop-high ropes course, by reservation
Toll Free (888) 800-9558
Phone (507) 467-2437
Email info@eagle-bluff.org
Web www.eagle-bluff.org

Eagle Cliff Campground
Canoe, kayak, innertube rentals
Phone (507) 467-2598
Web www.eaglecliff-campground.com

Scenic Valley Winery
Tasting, wine and gift shop
Toll Free (888) 965-0250
Phone (507) 467-2958
Fax (507) 467-2640

State Fish Hatchery
Largest trout hatchery in Minnesota.
Open Monday through Friday.
Phone (507) 467-3771
Email edstork@dnr.state.mn.us
Web www.dnr.state.mn.us

Peterson
1877 Peterson Station Museum
Phone (507) 875-2551

Geneva's Hideaway
Canoe and innertube rentals
Toll Free (877) 727-4816
Phone (507) 875-7733
Email genevas@acegroup.cc
Web www.genevashideaway.com

Rushford
Rushford Historic Depot
Depot, schoolhouse, church and jail
Phone (507) 864-7650

Whalan
May
Standstill Parade and Sykkle Tur
The parade doesn't move, the spectators do! Lefse and soapmaking demos, antique bicycles. Check website for date.
Toll Free (800) 944-2670
Phone (507) 467-2696
Web www.gatorgreens.net

ALTERNATE ACTIVITIES

Fountain
Fillmore County History Center
Collection of artifacts describing heritage of Fillmore County
Phone (507) 268-4449
Email fillmorehistory@earthlink.net
Web www.rootsweb.com/~mnfillmo

Houston
Houston Nature Center
REBART, recycled bike art weekend before labor Day, free nature programs every Saturday at 7:00 P.M., Restrooms, showers and visitor information on the Root River Trail
Phone (507) 896-4668
Email nature@acegroup.com
Web www.houstonmn.com

Lanesboro
Commonweal Theatre Company
Live professional theater, from Shakespeare to musicals, call for schedule
Toll Free (800) 657-7025
Phone (507) 467-2525
Email info@commonwealtheatre.org
Web www.commonwealtheatre.org

Cornicopia Art Center
Local and regional artists, year round exhibits
Phone (507) 467-2446
Email cac2446@acegroup.cc
Web www.lanesboroarts.org

Harmony-Preston Valley Trail

Vital Information:

Trail Distance: 18 miles

Trail Surface: asphalt

Access Points: Preston, Harmony, Root River Trail at Isinours Unit

Fees and Passes: none

Trail Website: www.dnr.state.mn

ABOUT THE TRAIL

A spur off the Root River Trail, it has enough character to merit independent status. The trail begins near the Isinours Unit near the west end of the Root River Trail and follows the south branch of the Root to Preston. From Preston it follows Camp Creek south for several miles then climbs quickly to the top of the ridge near Harmony. This trail crosses the creek many times and runs neither flat nor straight, making it a welcome addition to the trails of Minnesota.

TRAIL HIGHLIGHTS

Camp Creek is a quiet trout stream running through small woodlots and along the edge of farms and horse pastures. It's almost always shaded and quiet. Watch for small, seldom used concrete access bridges across the creek. If you don't feel up to climbing to Harmony, consider a bike shuttle to the town and an effortless ride down from the hilltop to the edge of Camp Creek. North of Preston, the trail has all the charm and more variety of terrain than any section of the Root River Trail. For a short side trip follow the 1 mile Trout Run Trail along the Root River in Preston.

ROAD HIGHLIGHTS

Highway 17 is recently paved and very smooth. It has moderate traffic and follows a scenic ridgeline until it drops into Preston. If you don't mind some gravel, ride Hwys 15 and 22 south from Preston. The route follows a valley creating an intimate, scenic ride. The gravel section is about 2 miles long on Hwy 22.

HOW TO GET THERE

Preston is about 40 miles south of Rochester on Hwy 52. Continue south on Highway 52 to Harmony for a hill-top start.

ABOUT THE ROADS

From hilltop to river bottom, expect a large change in elevation including either steep climbs or quick descents. Traffic on Hwy 22 near Harmony and Hwy 17 near Preston is moderate. Hwy 15 and the two mile section of Hwy 22 that is gravel are low traffic and very scenic.

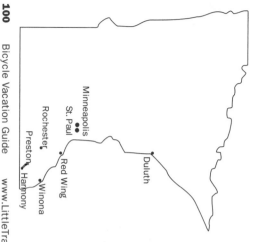

Southern Minnesota **Harmony-Preston Valley Trail**

Isinours to Harmony 17.6 miles

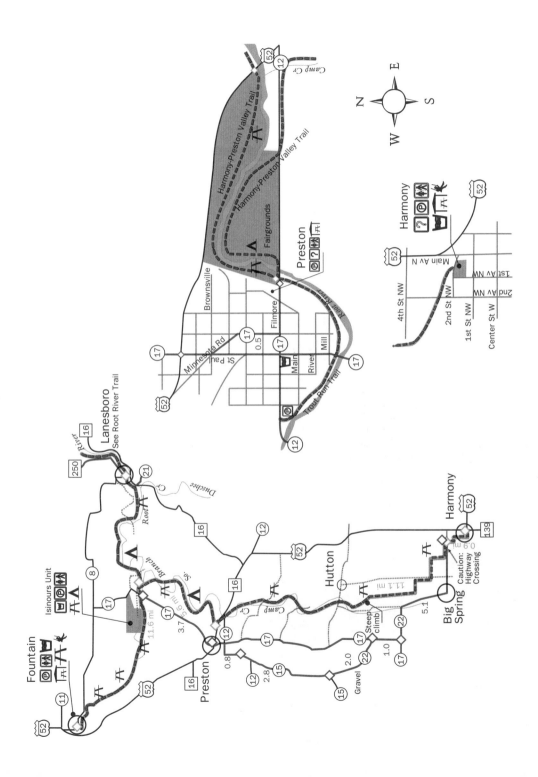

Harmony-Preston Valley Trail
Southern Minnesota

TOURIST INFORMATION

Harmony Visitor Information
Toll Free (800) 247-6466
Phone (507) 886-2469
Email visit@means.net
Web www.harmony.mn.us

Historic Forestville
Toll Free (888) 727-8386
Phone (507) 765-2785
Email forestville@mnhs.org
Web www.mnhs.org

Preston Area Tourism Association
Toll Free (888) 845-2100
Phone (507) 765-2100
Web www.preston.org

LODGING

Motels/Resorts

Harmony
Country Lodge Motel
PO Box 656
Toll Free (800) 870-1710
Phone (507) 886-2515

Preston
The Old Barn Resort
Rt3, Box 57
Toll Free (800) 552-2512
Phone (507) 467-2512
Web www.barnresort.com

Bed and Breakfast

Preston
Jailhouse Inn
109 Houston St NW
PO Box 422
Phone (507) 765-2181
Email sbinjail@rconnect.com
Web www.jailhouseinn.com

Camping

Harmony
Harmony Campground
Phone (507) 886-2469

Preston
Fillmore County Fairgrounds Camping
Phone (507) 765-2425

Maple Springs Campground, Inc.
RR2, Box 129B
Phone (507) 352-2056
Web www.exploreminnesota.com

The Old Barn Resort
Rt3, Box 57
Toll Free (800) 552-2512
Phone (507) 467-2512
Web www.barnresort.com

GROCERIES

Harmony
IGA
(507) 886-2225

Preston
IGA
(507) 765-2465

BIKE RENTAL

Harmony
Kingsley Merchantile
Phone (507) 886-2323

Preston
Brick House Coffee House
Toll Free (888) 999-1576
Phone (507) 765-9820
Email sendme@sendmeinminnesota.com
Web www.bluffcountry.com

Root River Outfitters
Phone (507) 467-2248

Southern Minnesota   Harmony-Preston Valley Trail

Photo by Vicky Vogels

Forestville

All Summer

Forestville Bread and Butter Day
Demonstrations of 1899 domestic arts
such as baking and butter making.
Check website for dates.
Toll Free (888) 727-8386
Phone (507) 765-2785
Web www.mnhs.org

July

4th of July at Forestville
Based on 4th of July in 1899, music,
speeches, children's games, Historic
Forestville, located in Forestville State
Park, First Weekend
Toll Free (888) 727-8386
Phone (507) 765-2785
Web www.mnhs.org

September

1899 Harvest Day
Saturday only, corn harvest, apple
cider pressing, quilting bee, heirloom
seed saving. Check website for date.
Toll Free (888) 727-8386
Phone (507) 765-2785
Web www.mnhs.org

Harmony

July

4th of July
Parade, kids' games, fireworks
Toll Free (800) 247-6466
Phone (507) 886-2469
Web www.harmony.mn.us

September

Fall Foliage Fest
Amish tours, horse and wagon rides,
scarecrow contest, toad races, sheep
shearing and spinning, fish fry at the
Legion, Fourth Weekend
Toll Free (800) 247-6466
Phone (507) 886-2469
Web www.harmony.mn.us

Preston

May

Trout Day and Sykkle Tur
Parade, bike ride, craft show, food
vendors, street dance, car show, Third
Weekend
Toll Free (888) 845-2100
Phone (705) 765-2100
Web www.preston.org

July

Fillmore County Fair
Exhibits, food, entertainment, Third
Weekend
Toll Free (888) 845-2100
Phone (507) 765-2100
Web www.preston.org

September

Fall Fest
Saturday only, hay wagon rides,
chicken BBQ, city wide garage sales,
Fourth Weekend
Toll Free (888) 845-2100
Phone (507) 765-2100
Web www.preston.org

Forestville

Forestville/Mystery Cave State Park
Trout fishing, camping, 17 mile shared
hiking and horseback trail system,
tours of Mystery Cave, the longest
cave in Minnesota
Phone (507) 352-5111
Fax (507) 352-5113
Web www.dnr.state.mn.us

Historic Forestville
Daily living history program with cos-
tumed interpreters, located in
Forestville State Park
Toll Free (888) 727-8386
Phone (507) 765-2785
Fax (507) 765-2785
Email forestville@mnhs.org
Web www.mnhs.org

Harmony

Amish Country Tours
Minibus and car tours of Amish farms
Phone (507) 886-2303
Email amish@means.net
Web www.shawcorp.com/amish

Photo by Vicky Vogels

Harmony-Preston Valley Trail Southern Minnesota

ALTERNATE ACTIVITIES cont'd

Austin's Goat Farm
200 baby angora goats produce mohair for knitters to create a variety of hand-crafted pieces, gift shop, tours
Phone (507) 886-6731
Email mohair@means.net
Web www.bluffcountry.com/austins.htm

Harmony Roller Rink
Indoor roller skating
Phone (507) 886-4444

Harmony Toy Museum
Over 4,000 toys on display
Phone (507) 867-3380

Michel's Amish Tours
Personal guide through Amish country
Toll Free (800) 752-6474
Phone (507) 886-5392
Web
www.bluffcountry.com/michel.htm

Niagara Cave
Daily guided tours, 60 foot under-ground waterfall, gift shop
Toll Free (800) 837-6606
Phone (507) 886-6606
Email niagara@means.net
Web www.niagaracave.com

Slim's Wood Shed
Woodcarving museum/workshop, hand carved circus caricatures dis-play, woodcarving supplies and gift shop
Phone (507) 886-3114
Email slims_ws@means.net
Web www.web-site.com/slimswood-shed/

Preston

Amish Tours
Personal or group tours to Amish homes, including furniture and basket making demonstrations, quilts and produce for sale
Phone (507) 765-2477

Preston Apple and Berry Farm
Apples, cider, baked goods, bedding plants through June, pick your own strawberries June and July
Phone (507) 765-4486

Photo by Vicky Vogels

Photo by Vicky Vogels

Madeline Island Trail

Vital Information:

Trail Distance: 6 miles

Trail Surface: paved

Access Points: LaPointe

Fees and Passes: none

Trail Website: madelineisland.com

ABOUT THE TRAIL

Madeline Island is three miles off the shores of Bayfield, Wisconsin, in the heart of the Apostle Islands of Lake Superior. Access via a ferry. Explore the island town of LaPointe, then circle the island for great views of Lake Superior and intimate wanders through deep forest. Lake Superior chills the island through June. Best times to visit are July through September.

TRAIL HIGHLIGHTS

There is no formal trail through Madeline Island, but a paved shoulder on Middle Road is designated for bikes only and leads to the most popular destination on the Island, Big Bay State Park.

ABOUT THE ROADS

Madeline Island is almost flat, with a few small rises. Traffic is restricted to 40 miles per hour on the whole island and the speed limit is generally observed. The roads have low traffic, are well maintained and wander through dense forest and along the shores of Lake Superior.

ROAD HIGHLIGHTS

Big Bay Road, between Big Bay Town Park and School House Road, has the best views of Lake Superior. South Shore Drive is quiet and remote as it wanders through deep woods. The park roads in Big Bay State Park are scenic and low traffic. North Shore Drive and the roads connecting to it are gravel. The surface is generally well maintained, but wide tires are recommended. The island has approximately 30 miles of roads and most are worth riding.

HOW TO GET THERE

Take I-35 to Duluth and cross into Wisconsin on Hwy 2. Go east on Hwy 2 to Hwy 13 south and follow Hwy 13 around the Bayfield Peninsula to Bayfield. Take the Madeline Island Ferry from Bayfield to the Island. Hwy 63 through northwest Wisconsin offers a more direct route, but it is usually two lanes and runs through numerous small towns.

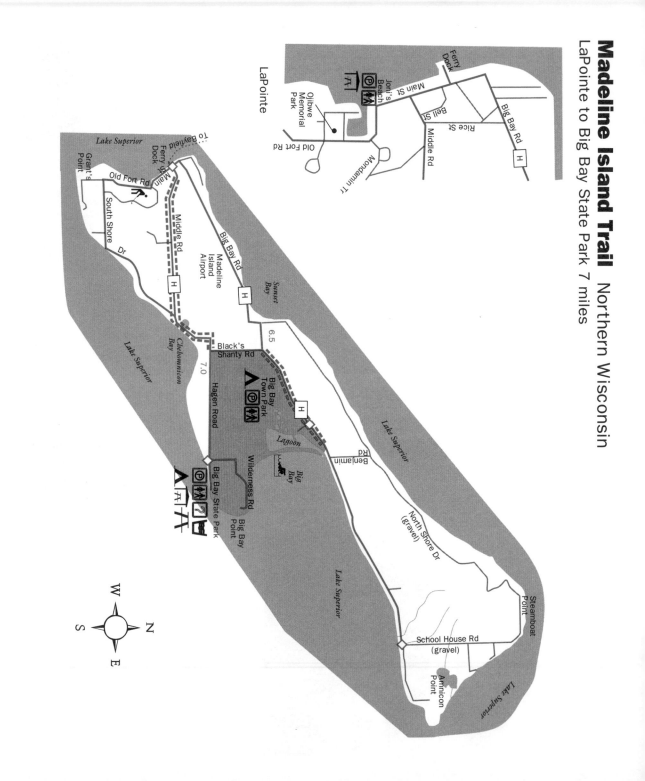

Madeline Island Trail

LaPointe to Big Bay State Park 7 miles

Northern Wisconsin

TOURIST INFORMATION

Bayfield Chamber of Commerce
Toll Free (800) 447-4094
Phone (715) 779-5080
Email bayfieldchamber@charter.net
Web www.bayfield.org

Madeline Island Chamber of Commerce
Toll Free (888) 475-3386
Phone (715) 747-2801
Email vacation@madelineisland.com
Web www.madelineisland.com

Madeline Island Ferry Service
Phone (715) 747-2051
Email vacation@madelineisland.com
Web http://www.madferry.com

LODGING

Motels/Resorts

Bayfield

Harbor's Edge Motel
331 N Front Street
Phone (715) 779-3926
Email info@harborsedgemotel.com
Web www.harborsedgemotel.com

LaPointe

Madeline Island Motel
P.O. Box 51
Phone (715) 747-3000
Fax (715) 747-3003
Email mimotel@aol.com

The Inn on Madeline Island
PO Box 93
Toll Free (800) 822-6315
Fax (715) 747-6345
Email theinn@madisland.com
Web www.madisland.com

Bed and Breakfast

Bayfield

Apostle Island Rentals
Toll Free (800) 842-1199

Phone (715) 779-3621
Web www.apostleisland.com

Bay Front Inn
15 Front Street
Toll Free (888) 243-4191
Phone (715) 779-3880
Web www.explorewisconsin.com

Greunke's First St. Inn
17 Rittenhouse Avenue
Phone (715) 779-5480
Email judith@greunkesinn.com
Web www.greunkesinn.com

Isaac Wing House
17 South First Street
Toll Free (888) 320-5468
Phone (715) 779-3907
Email iwh@cheqnet.net
Web www.isaacwinghouse.com

Old Rittenhouse Inn
301 Rittenhouse Avenue
Toll Free (888) 644-4667
Phone (715) 779-5111
Web www.rittenhouseinn.com

Pilot House Inn
101 Washington
Phone (715) 779-3561
Email Gunderson@PilotHouseInn.com
Web www.pilothouseinn.com

The Bayfield Inn
20 Rittenhouse Avenue
Toll Free (800) 382-0995
Phone (715) 779-3363
Email bayinn@cheqnet.net
Web www.thebayfieldinn.com

Washington Condos
c/o Winfield Inn
Washington Ave & 1st Street
Phone (715) 779-3252
Email info@winfieldinn.com
Web www.winfieldinn.com

LaPointe

Bog Lake Outfitters
P. O. Box 341
Phone (715) 747-2685
Email boglakeotftr@yahoo.com
Web www.madelineisland.com/boglake

Brittany Cottages
Old Fort Road
P.O. Box 458
Phone (715) 747-5023
Fax (715) 747-6263
Email brittany@cheqnet.net
Web http://www.brittanycabins.com

Cadotte's Cottages
P.O. Box 103A
Phone (715) 743-3075
Email cado@cheqnet.net

Madeline Island Rentals
Toll Free (888) 747-5775
Phone (715) 747-5775
Email stay@madelineislandrentals.com
Web www.madelineislandrentals.com

Marshcroft on Madeline Island
1360 Middle Road
Toll Free (800) 243-5283
Phone (715) 747-5555
Fax (715) 747-5405
Email nwcoftsp@nwcoffeemills.com
Web www.marshcroft.com

Madeline Island Trail

Northern Wisconsin

Email vacation@madelineisland.com
Web www.madelineisland.com

Old LaPointe Inn
197 Big Bay Road
Phone (715) 747-2628
Fax (715) 747-2629
Email escape@lapointeinn.com
Web http://www.lapointeinn.com

Smith's Whose House
Phone (715) 747-3613
Email marjoriesmith@mac.com
Web homepage.mac.com/
marjoriesmith

White Seagull B&B
Toll Free (800) 977-2624
Phone (715) 747-5135
Email isrental@ncis.net
Web http://www.islandrental.com

Woods Manor
P.O. Box 7
Toll Free (800) 966-3756
Email tundra@islandelegance.com
Web http://www.islandelegance.com

Camping

Bayfield

Apostle Islands Area Campground
85150 Trailer Ct Rd
Phone (715) 779-5524

Dalrymple Park
Bayfield City Hall
North Highway 13
Phone (715) 779-5712

La Pointe

Big Bay State Park
P.O. Box 589
Toll Free (800) 947-2757
Phone (715) 747-6425
Email Mark.Eggleson@dnr.state.wi.us
Web www.reserveamerica.com

Big Bay Town Park
Toll Free (888) 475-3386
Phone (715) 747-2801

GROCERIES

Bayfield

Andy's IGA Foodliner
(715) 779-5415

LaPointe

Island Store
(715) 747-6635

Lori's Store
(715) 747-5200

BIKE RENTAL

Bayfield

Trek & Trail
Toll Free (800) 354-8735
Phone (715) 779-3595
Email trek@scc.net
Web www.trek-trail.com

LaPointe

Motion to Go
Phone (715) 747-6585
Email drgoldo@cheqnet.net

BIKE REPAIR

Ashland

Bay City Cycles
Phone (715) 682-2091

FESTIVALS AND EVENTS

Bayfield

May

Bayfield in Bloom
A month-long celebration of blooming
wildflowers and orchards, Mid May
through Mid June
Toll Free (800) 447-4094
Phone (715) 779-5080
Web www.bayfield.org

June

Lake Superior Big Top Chautauqua
850 seat tent theatre. A 70 night summer season of concerts, variety shows and original historical musicals including national acts. Summer schedule runs from mid-June to early September
Toll Free (888) 244-8368
Phone (715) 373-5552
Web www.bigtop.org

On the Water Celebration
Four day Inland Sea Symposium on conservation & kayaking-field trips, speakers and workshops, Blessing of the Fleet ecumenical blessing for watercraft. Around the Island Sailboat Race, Call for dates.
Toll Free (800) 447-4094
Phone (715) 779-5080
Web www.bayfield.org

July

Fourth of July Celebrations
Fireworks and strawberry shortcake social, parade, live music, speeches, Fireworks on Madeline Island.
Toll Free (800) 447-4094
Phone (715) 779-5080
Web www.bayfield.org

August

Art on the Lake Celebration
Multiple festivals rolled into one. Art auction, Bayfield Fine Arts & Craft Show, Artist's Gallery Walk, Red Cliff Cultural Days & Native American Music Fest, in Bayfield's Waterfront Park. First Weekend
Toll Free (800) 447-4094
Phone (715) 779-5080
Web www.bayfield.org

September

Apostle Annual Lighthouse Celebration
Three weeks of special lighthouse cruises and lighthouse tours, featuring all seven historic lighthouses of the Apostle Islands. Begins the Wednesday after Labor Day
Toll Free (800) 779-4487
Phone (715) 779-5619
Web www.lighthousecelebration.com

October

Bayfield Apple Festival
During the peak of fall color; orchard growers, artists, musicians and creative kids' activities. Wide variety of apple treats plus arts and crafts fair, First Weekend
Toll Free (800) 447-4094
Phone (715) 779-5080
Web www.bayfield.org

LaPointe

October

Madeline Island Fall Festival
Local artist displays, demonstrations, pumpkin carving, kids costume parade, celebration of fall colors, community and art. Call for date.
Toll Free (888) 475-3386
Web www.madelineisland.com

Bayfield

Adventures in Perspective
Specializing in guided trips and kayak rentals in the Apostle Islands National Lakeshore; instructional clinics, half-day, full day, and overnight extended tours, Ferry pick-ups available.
Phone (715) 779-9503
Email info@livingadventure.com
Web http://www.livingadventure.com

Apostle Islands National Lakeshore
Visit the other 21 Apostle Islands, pristine sand beaches, spectacular sea caves, old-growth forests, bald eagles, black bears and the largest collection of lighthouses anywhere in the National Park System. Great sailing, boating, kayaking, and hiking. Permits are required for camping and reservations are recommended. The visitor center is a short walk from the Bayfield end of the ferry.
Phone (715) 779-3397
Email APIS_Webmaster@nps.gov
Web http://www.nps.gov/apis

Bayfield Apple Company
State's largest raspberry crop. Pick raspberries in the summer, taste apples in the fall, and purchase ciders, jams, jellies and fruit butters.
Toll Free (800) 363-4526
Phone (715) 779-5700
Email orchard@bayfieldapple.com
Web www.bayfieldapple.com

Madeline Island Trail   Northern Wisconsin

Bayfield Maritime Museum
150 years of Bayfield history with hands-on demonstrations of commercial fishing, boat building, lighthouses, sailor crafts and shipwrecks
Phone (715) 779-9919
Web www.apostleisland.com

Farmers Market
Corner of 3rd and Manypenny, Saturday mornings from mid June to mid October

Guided Walking Tour by Lantern Light
90 minute tour that captures the history and romance of old Bayfield. Visit 24 historic sites listed on the National Register, learn the early history from 1856-1920's. Hear tales of fortunes gained & lost.
Phone (715) 779-0299

Trek & Trail
A variety of day and overnight kayak guided trips around the Apostle Islands National Lakeshore. See sea caves, secluded white sand beaches, old shipwrecks, historic lighthouses and a variety of wildlife.
Toll Free (800) 354-8735
Phone (715) 779-3595
Email trek@scc.net
Web www.trek-trail.com

LaPointe

Apostle Island Cruise Service
Choose from a variety of narrated cruises including island shuttles, sunset cruises, and lighthouse tours.
Toll Free (800) 323-7619
Phone (715) 779-3925
Email info@apostleisland.com
Web www.apostleisland.com/main.htm

Big Bay State Park
1.5 mile sandy beach, picnic area, more than 9 miles of hiking trails, bird and wildlife watching. Interpretive programs during summer months.
Phone (715) 747-6425
Email Mark.Eggleson@dnr.state.wi.us
Web www.dnr.state.wi.us

Bog Lake Outfitters
Canoe, paddle and rowboat rentals. At Big Bay Town Park for use in the lagoon.
Phone (715) 747-2685
Email boglakeotftr@yahoo.com
Web www.madelineisland.com/boglake

Capser & Meech Hiking Trails
The Madeline Island Wilderness Preserve; inland forest land for public enjoyment; Capser & Meech, two rustic, ungroomed trails, are approximately half a mile from the ferry.
Toll Free (888) 475-3386
Phone (715) 747-2801
Email vacation@madelineisland.com
Web www.madelineisland.com

LaPointe Center Art Guilde & Gallery
Showcases local and regional artists in a variety of mediums. Summer lectures, films and gallery exhibits
Phone (715) 747-3321

Madeline Island Historical Museum
Prehistoric relics from the days of Ojibwe habitation, trade goods, missionaries' effects, tools of the lumbering and maritime industries.
Phone (715) 747-2415
Email madeline@whs.wisc.edu
Web www.wisconsinhistory.org

Sandstrom Center for the Arts
Art classes and workshops for children and adults.
Phone (715) 747-2054

Gandy Dancer Trail

Vital Information:

Trail Distance: 47 miles

Trail Surface: limestone

Access Points: St. Croix Falls, Centuria, Milltown, Luck, Frederic, Lewis, Siren, Webster, Danbury

Fees and Passes: Wisconsin State Trail Pass; $3 daily fee or $10 for an annual pass. State Trail passes are good on all Wisconsin State Trails.

Trail Website:
http://www.polkcountytourism.com

ABOUT THE TRAIL

This former SOO Line railroad bed follows Highway 35 from St. Croix Falls to Danbury. Small towns dot the trail at 4 to 7 mile intervals providing plenty of access points and opportunities to start or stop. I saw more variety of wildlife on this trail than any other, in part because I rode sections in a light rain when no one else was on the trail.

TRAIL HIGHLIGHTS

Frederic has endorsed the trail. The town has rebuilt the historic depot and developed other facilities for bicyclists. Coon Lake Park, about half a mile east of the trail in Frederic, offers a shady, restful lakeside stop. See city map. The trail skirts several lakes and passes through bogs and cattail marshes for several miles north and south of Siren. At the far north end, the trail makes a high crossing of the Yellow River just south of Danbury. Although the improved surface ends at Hwy 77 in Danbury, it is worth walking or riding a fat tired bike 0.4 miles north to the bridge over the St. Croix River. The bridge, about 300 feet long and 100 feet above the river, overlooks a pristine portion of the St. Croix. ATVs and other motorized vehicles are allowed on this stretch, so proceed with caution.

ABOUT THE ROADS

Polk and Burnett counties offer a wide selection of beautiful, low traffic roads. Northern roads wind around

lakes and weave through forests. Southern roads undulate through a mix of farmland and woodlots. Hills can be long, but the grade is usually mild to intermediate. Ride one way on the trail and return by the roads for an interesting mix of scenery and topography.

ROAD HIGHLIGHTS

The eastern route between Luck and Centuria or St. Croix Falls offers a diverse, alternative to the flat and straight trail. The east and west loops between Danbury and Oakland skirt lakes, meander through a full canopy of tree crowns and generally take in a wide range of lakes and northwoods beauty. Expect rolling hills, but not a lot of dramatic climbs and descents.

HOW TO GET THERE

St. Croix Falls is about an hour from the Twin Cities. Take Interstate 35 north to Highway 8. Go east into Wisconsin. Turn south on Highway 35, toward Interstate Park, and stop at the Polk County Information Center just off the ramp. Trail begins at the information center. For mid-trail towns, stay on Highway 8 to Highway 35 north and pick up the trail at any one of the towns along the highway. Danbury, on the north end of the trail, can also be reached by taking Interstate 35 to Hinckley and heading east on Highway 48. Highway 48 becomes Highway 77 in Wisconsin.

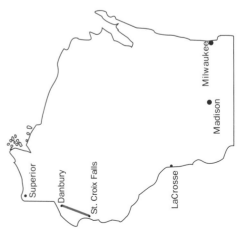

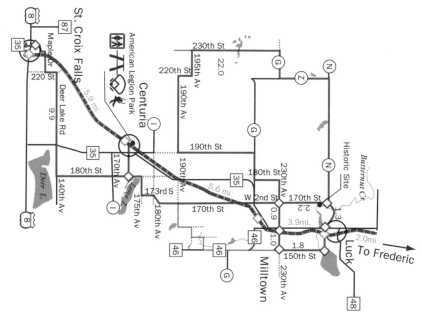

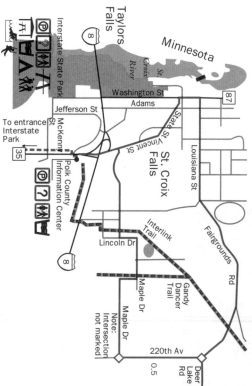

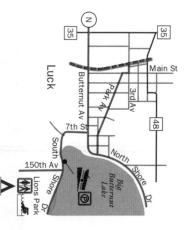

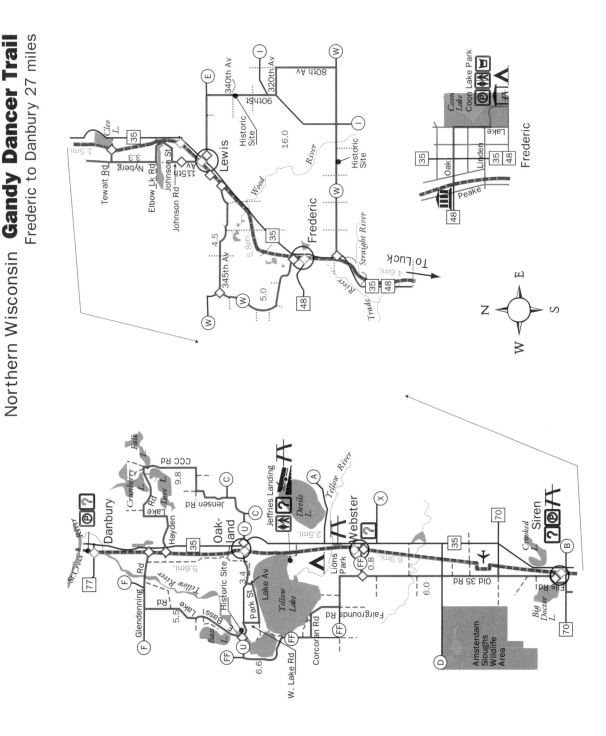

Gandy Dancer Trail Northern Wisconsin

Burnett County Tourism Dept
Toll Free (800) 788-3164
Phone (715) 349-5999
Email bctour@sirentel.net
Web www.burnettcounty.com

Frederic Village Hall
Phone (715) 327-4836
Web www.frederic-wi.com

Luck Village Hall
Phone (715) 472-2221
Web www.polkcountytourism.com

Polk County Information, St. Croix Falls
Toll Free (800) 222-7655
Phone (715) 483-1410
Email polkinfo@lakeland.ws
Web www.polkcountytourism.com

Village of Centuria
Phone (715) 646-2300
Email info@centuria-wi.org
Web www.centuria-wi.org

Webster Area Chamber of Commerce
Toll Free (800) 788-3194
Phone (715) 866-4211
Email fun@websterwisconsin.com
Web www.websterwisconsin.com

LODGING

Motels/Resorts

Luck
Luck Country Inn
Hwy 35 & 48
Toll Free (800) 544-7396
Phone (715) 472-2000
Web www.luckcountryinn.com

Siren
Best Western Northwoods Lodge
Jct Highway 35 & 70
Toll Free (877) 349-7800

The Lodge at Crooked Lake
24271 State Road 35 N
Toll Free (877) 843-5634

St. Croix Falls
Holiday Inn Express Hotel & Suites
2190 US Hwy 8
Toll Free (877) 422-4097
Phone (715) 483-5775

Bed and Breakfast

Osceola
Pleasant Lake Bed & Breakfast
2238 60th Ave
Toll Free (800) 294-2545
Phone (715) 294-2545
Web www.pleasantlake.com

St. Croix Falls
Wissahickon Farms Country Inn
2263 Maple Drive
Phone (715) 483-3986

Taylors Falls
High Woods B&B
35930 Wild Mountain Road
Phone (651) 465-5307
Email highwood@scc.net
Web www.highwoods.net

The Cottage B&B
950 Fox Glen Drive, Box 71
Phone (651) 465-3595
Web www.the-cottage.com

The Old Jail B&B
349 Government St

PO Box 203
Phone (651) 465-3112
Email oldjail@scc.net
Web www.oldjail.com

Camping

St Croix Falls
Interstate State Park Campground
Hwy 35
Phone (715) 483-3747

Taylors Falls
Wildwood Campground
PO Box 235
Toll Free (800) 447-4958
Phone (651) 465-6315
Email fun@wildmountain.com
Web www.wildmountain.com

Webster
DuFour's Pine Tree Campground
PO Box 335
Phone (715) 656-4084

GROCERIES

Danbury
Wayne's Foods Plus
(715) 656-3456

Luck
Natural Alternative Food Co-op
(715) 472-8084

GROCERIES cont'd

Wayne's Foods Plus
(715) 472-2210

Milltown
Dick's Food Pride
(715) 825-2200

Siren
R & M Foods
(715) 349-5656

St. Croix Falls
Marketplace
(715) 483-5178

Webster
Wayne's Foods Plus
(715) 866-8366

BIKE RENTAL

St. Croix Falls
Wissahickon Farms Country Inn
Phone (715) 483-3986

BIKE REPAIR

St. Croix Falls
Wissahickon Farms Country Inn
Phone (715) 483-3986

FESTIVALS AND EVENTS

Centuria
July
Centuria Memory Days
Parade, softball tournaments, craft
fair, street dance, tractor pull, classic
car show, First Weekend
Toll Free (800) 222-7655
Phone (715) 646-2300
Web www.centuria-wi.org

Frederic
June
Frederic Lions Bike Race and Tour
38 mile race on the scenic back roads
around Frederic, 5km walk and run.
Check website for date.
Phone (715) 327-4256
Web www.fredericlionsclassic.com

July
Indianhead Gem & Mineral Show
Local artists showing jewelry, raw and
polished rocks at the high school,
Third Weekend
Toll Free (800) 222-7655
Phone (715) 327-4836
Web www.frederic-wi.com

October
Mixed Sampler Guild Quilt Show
Over 50 quilters from multiple states,
at the High School, Second Weekend
Phone (800) 222-7655
Web www.frederic-wi.com

Luck
July
Lucky Days Celebration
"In and Out of Luck" Run/Race/Walk,
parade, midway, food, street dance,
Third Weekend
Toll Free (800) 222-7655
Web www.polkcountytourism.com

Milltown
June
Fisherman's Party
Parade, food and horseshoe pitching
contests, Third Weekend
Phone (800) 222-7655
Web www.polkcountytourism.com

Siren
July
Fourth of July Celebration
5K run/walk, bed race, parade, boat
parade, fireworks, First Weekend
Toll Free (800) 788-3164
Phone (715) 349-5999
Web www.burnettcounty.com

August
Summer Fest
Sidewalk sale, arts and crafts, softball
tournament, volleyball tournament,
kiddie parade, street dance and
chicken BBQ, First Weekend
Toll Free (800) 788-3164
Phone (715) 349-5999
Web www.burnettcounty.com

Gandy Dancer Trail Northern Wisconsin

St. Croix Falls

July

Polk County Fair

Horse shows, live entertainment, tractor and truck pulls, carnival rides, farm animals, Fourth Weekend

Toll Free (800) 222-7655

Web www.polkcountytourism.com

Wannigan Days

Parade, fireworks, queen coronation, craft show, Centered on lumberjack era, Second Weekend

Toll Free (800) 222-7655

Web www.polkcountytourism.com

Webster

August

Gandy Dancer Days

Street dance, queen pageant, sidewalk sales, Second Weekend

Phone (715) 788-3164

Toll Free (800) 349-5999

Web www.burnettcounty.com

Balsam Lake

Polk County Museum

Native American and lumbering era artifacts

Phone (715) 485-9269

Web www.co.polk.wi.us/museum

Grantsburg

Crex Meadows Wildlife Area

2,399 acre refuge of prairie and wetlands, see sandhill cranes, bald and golden eagles, thousands of ducks and geese, Extensive road system and well marked informational and directional signs

Phone (715) 463-2739

Web www.crexmeadows.org

Osceola

Osceola & St. Croix Valley Railway

Experience rail travel as it was during the first half of the century. 1916 redbrick depot, train rides every weekend May through October

Toll Free (715) 711-2591

Email oscvrlwy@centurytel.net

Web www.trainride.org

St. Croix Falls

Interstate Park

Wisconsin's oldest state park; camping, hiking, interpretive center and stunning views of the scenic St. Croix River

Phone (715) 483-3747

Email wiparks@dnr.state.wi.us

Web www.dnr.state.wi.us

St. Croix Festival Theater

Non-profit professional theater productions of classical, contemporary and forgotten works, May through December

Toll Free (888) 887-6002

Phone (715) 483-3387

Email info@festivaltheatre.org

Web www.festivaltheatre.org

St.Croix National Scenic Riverway Visitor's Center

Traces the wild St. Croix and Namekagon Rivers for more than 250 miles, staff will help plan canoe trips

Phone (715) 483-3284

Web www.nps.gov/saan

Taylors Falls

Taylors Falls Scenic Boat Tours

Four trips daily down the St. Croix River. June through August

Toll Free (800) 447-4958

Phone (651) 465-6315

Email fun@wildmountain.com

Web www.wildmountain.com

Wild Mountain

Waterslides, Alpine Slides Go-Karts and Canoe Rental

Toll Free (800) 447-4958

Phone (651) 465-6315

Email fun@wildmountain.com

Web www.wildmountain.com

Webster

Forts Folle Avoine Historical Park

Reconstructed 1802 Fur Trade Post, 80 acres of hiking along the Yellow River

Phone (715) 866-8890

Email use website

Web www.theforts.org

Old Abe Trail

Vital Information:

Trail Distance: 20 miles

Trail Surface: asphalt

Access Points: Lake Wissota, Jim Falls, Cornell, Brunet Island State Park

Fees and Passes: Wisconsin State Trail Pass; $3 daily fee or $10 for an annual pass. State Trail passes are good on all Wisconsin State Trails.

Trail Website: www.chippewa-wi.com

ABOUT THE TRAIL

With a state park at either end, the undeveloped shores of the Chippewa River near the middle and a mix of hardwood forests and agriculture for its entire length, this trail offers a scenic look at an attractive part of western Wisconsin. The trail name comes from Old Abe, a bald eagle that became the mascot of Company C of the 8th Wisconsin Infantry during the Civil War.

TRAIL HIGHLIGHTS

The middle section, just north of Jim Falls, skirts the edge of Old Abe Lake then passes through a forest of oak, birch, maple and cherry. Look upriver, at the small bridge over the pond, for a picturesque view of the Coban Bridge, a 1906 overhead truss bridge. The bridge was moved to this spot during the winters of 1916 and 1917 by horse and sled when the Wissota Dam was built. The 175 foot steel structure in Cornell is the only known pulpwood stacker in the world. The visitor center at the base describes the history and operation of the stacker. The trail extends to Brunet Island State Park near Cornell. Follow the trail to the Park, then ride the 3 mile park road as it circles the island.

ABOUT THE ROADS

This is flat to rolling land. Expect a low to moderate roller coaster ride as you move toward or away from the river. The routes flatten out in the river floodplain and beyond the valley. Agricultural fields are small to mid-sized and intermingled with woodlots.

Traffic is generally very low as long as you stay away from main connector routes like Cty S and the State Highways. Hwy 178 on the west side of the Chippewa River is very scenic, but traffic is high and fast and the road is narrow, not recommended.

ROAD HIGHLIGHTS

The park road in Brunet Island State Park circles the island under a canopy of evergreens. Allow time for frequent stops at beaches and picnic grounds. This is a very peaceful road where bikes generally travel as fast as automobiles. County Road K, north of the Coban Bridge, is closer to the river and offers a better view than the trail. For a unique experience, cross the one way Coban Bridge. The deck is wood and planks have been laid in two rows at the width of auto tires. A marker just south of the bridge highlights its history. Use caution when crossing Hwy 178 to get to the marker.

HOW TO GET THERE

From the Twin Cities, take I-94 east to the Hwy 29/40 exit, east of Menomonie. Follow Hwy 29 east to Hwy 53, on the western edge of Chippewa Falls. Go north approximately 3 miles to Cty Rd S and turn right. Go east 5.5 miles on S to the intersection of County Roads S and O. The trailhead is on the north side of Cty Rd S. Stay on Cty Rd S to Jim Falls for a mid-trail start, or go through Jim Falls to Hwy 27 then north on Hwy 27 to Cornell to start at Brunet Island State Park.

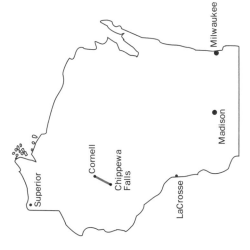

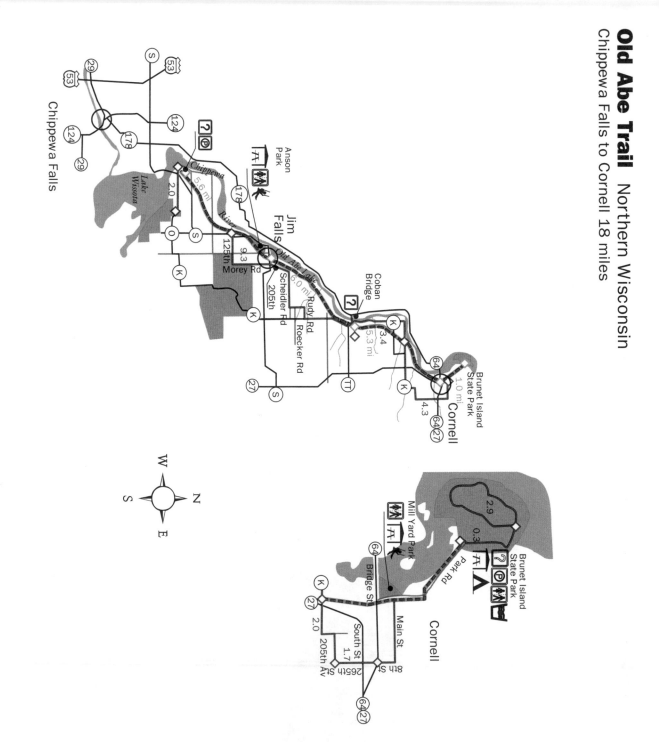

Northern Wisconsin Old Abe Trail

TOURIST INFORMATION

Chippewa Falls Area Visitors Center
Toll Free (866) 723-0340
Phone (715) 723-0331
Email info@chippewachamber.org
Web www.chippewachamber.org

Cornell Development Association, Inc
Toll Free (866) 723-0331
Phone (715) 239-3717
Web www.cityofcornell.com

LODGING

Motels/Resorts

Chippewa Falls
HideAway Resort
5967 167th St
Phone (715) 720-7367

Cornell
Edgewater Motel
24250 state Hwy 178
Phone (715) 239-6295

Bed and Breakfast

Chippewa Falls
McGilvray's Victorian B&B
312 W. Columbia St.
Toll Free (888) 324-1893
Phone (715) 720-1600

Pleasant View B&B
16649 96th Ave
Toll Free (866) 947-7682

Phone (715) 382-4401
Web www.pleasantviewbb.com

Holcombe
The Happy Horse B & B
24469 Hwy 27
Phone (715) 239-0707
Email happyhorsebb@centurytel.net
Web www.happyhorsebb.com

Camping

Chippewa Falls
Lake Wissota State Park
18127 Co Hwy O
Phone (715) 382-4574
Web www.dnr.state.wi.us

Pine Harbor Campground
7181 185 St
Phone (715) 723-9865

Cornell
Brunet Island State Park
23125 255th St.
Phone (715) 239-6888

GROCERIES

Chippewa Falls
Gordy's County Market
(715) 726-2500

Sokup's Market
(715) 723-4953

Cornell
Super Value
(715) 239-6833

Jim Falls
Cenex Convenience Mart

Lake Wissota
Gordy's County Market
(715) 726-2505

BIKE REPAIR

Chippewa Falls
Spring Street Sports
Phone (715) 723-6616

FESTIVALS AND EVENTS

Chippewa Falls

May

Leinenkugel Chippewa Valley Century Ride
Begins and ends in Irvine Park, with 25, 50, 75 , 100 mile stages. Brat Feed at end. Memorial Day Weekend.
Phone (715) 723-5557
Web www.chippewavalleyride.us

July

Northern Wisconsin State Fair
Midway, free grandstand show, livestock, crafts. Check website for dates.
Toll Free (866) 723-0340
Phone (715) 723-2861
Web www.chippewachamber.org

August

Chip Dip
Tube float down the Chippewa River, Third Weekend
Phone (715) 723-5667
Web www.chippewachamber.org

Old Abe Trail Northern Wisconsin

FESTIVALS AND EVENTS cont'd

Tour de Chippewa Bike Ride 32, 60, or 100 mile routes starting and ending in Irvine Park. Check website for date.
Toll Free (877) 945-3379
Web www.chippewachamber.org

September

Oktoberfest
Family fun, German food, 3 stages with music, beer gardens. Held at the Northern Wisconsin Fair Grounds. Check website for date.
Phone (715) 723-0340
Toll Free (866) 723-0331
Web www.chippewachamber.org

Cornell

June

Cornell Community Fair
Parade, live music, Lion's Club Chicken BBQ, Mill Yard Park, First Weekend
Toll Free (866) 723-0331
Phone (715) 239-3717
Web www.cityofcornell.com

July

July 3rd Fireworks
Lion's Club BBQ chicken, Mill Yard Park. Held the night before the 4th.
Toll Free (866) 723-0331
Phone (715) 239-3717
Web www.cityofcornell.com

October

Pork in the Park Polka
Roasted pork dinner, homemade pies, activities for children, Polka Band and dance contest, Mill Yard Park, First Weekend
Toll Free (866) 723-0331
Phone (715) 239-3717
Web www.cityofcornell.com

ALTERNATE ACTIVITIES

Chippewa Falls Museum of Industry & Technology
History of local manufacturing and processing from 1840's to present including Cray Super Computer collection,
Phone (715) 720-9206
Web www.chippewachamber.org

Cook Rutledge Mansion
Fine example of High Victorian Italianate architecture
Phone (715) 723-7181
Web www.chippewachamber.org

Heyde Center for the Arts
Renovated High School, live theater, musical performances, art shows, dance and festivals
Phone (715) 726-9000
Email cvca@cvol.net
Web www.cvca.net

Historic Walking Tour of Downtown Chippewa Falls
Listed on the National Register of Historic Places, 36 historic buildings and points of interest,
Toll Free (866) 723-0340
Phone (715) 723-7858
Web www.chippewachamber.org

Irvine Park and Zoo
225 acres of natural wooded areas, Zoo, hiking, picnicking, playgrounds, School House Museum and Norwegian Log Home
Phone (715) 723-0051

Lake Wissota State Park
Hiking, biking, camping, swimming
Phone (715) 382-4574
Email wiparks@dnr.state.wi.us
Web www.dnr.state.wi.us

Leinenkugel's Brewery Tours
Half hour tours until 3:00 P.M. every day through summer, closed Sundays after Labor Day.
Toll Free (888) 534-6437
Phone (715) 723-5557
Web www.leinie.com

Rose Garden/Lily Garden
Gardener's paradise. 500 roses, teas, floribunda, grandifloras, miniatures and climbers. Located at corner of Bridge St & Jefferson Ave.
Phone (715) 723-0051

Cornell

Brunet Island State Park
Island Park in the Chippewa River, scenic drive, camping, swimming and hiking
Phone (715) 239-6888
Web www.cityofcornell.com

Mill Yard Park
175 foot high wood stacker used from 1913 to 1972, only known pulp wood stacker in the world, visitor's center
Toll Free (866) 723-0331
Phone (715) 239-3717
Web www.cityofcornell.com

Red Cedar Trail

Vital Information:

Trail Distance: 14 miles

Trail Surface: limestone

Access Points: Menomonie, Irvington, Downsville

Fees and Passes: Wisconsin State Trail Pass; $3 daily fee or $10 for an annual pass. State Trail passes are good on all Wisconsin State Trails.

Trail Website: www.dnr.state.wi.us

ABOUT THE TRAIL

This attractive trail has the feel of a Victorian era carriage road next to a canal. Downsville, at the midpoint, is an excellent starting or turn-around point for those who don't want to ride the entire trail. The Creamery, in Downsville, is a fine dining restaurant with screened in patio and wildflower gardens. The trail enters the Dunnville Wildlife Area near its southern tip, a wetland prairie in the Chippewa River floodplain. The southern end of the trail connects with the Chippewa State Trail after crossing the Chippewa River on an 860 foot railroad trestle.

ROAD HIGHLIGHTS

Hardscrabble Road, south of Downsville, is also hard climbing if traveling south to north. Hardscrabble is shady and lightly traveled, has excellent pavement and offers a couple of great views of the river valley to the west. If you are looking for a short diversion from the trail, this is the road to take. County Roads C and D offer a couple of steep climbs near the river, then rolling, rural panoramic views. Paradise Valley Road parallels the trail north of Irvington from a vantage point slightly inland and higher, a quiet road with low underbrush on both sides and occasional views of the river.

TRAIL HIGHLIGHTS

Its hard to go wrong on this trail. From Menomonie to Downsville the trail and river run right next to each other. Watch for the historic site of the Downsville Cut Stone Company about two and a half miles south of Downsville. Go another mile south and enter a very remote and beautiful stretch of river. The prairie portion of the Dunnville Wildlife Area radiates a wonderful purple hue in late August. Closer to the river, the vegetation changes to erratic clumps of brush in an ever-shifting sandy shoreline. The trestle bridge offers great views of the river.

HOW TO GET THERE

Menomonie is about 30 miles west of Eau Claire on Interstate 94. Take the Highway 25 exit south off Interstate 94. Go south about 2.5 miles to Highway 29 west. Go west on Highway 29 about one half mile. The trailhead is on the left side of the road just after crossing the Red Cedar River. See City map for details. Continue south on Hwy 25 about 6 miles to Downsville.

ABOUT THE ROADS

Expect a mix of woods and farmland and low to medium rollers. Traffic is low to medium on the county roads and slightly higher on the short stretches of State Highways, such as Highway 72 near Downsville. The steepest terrain is near the river.

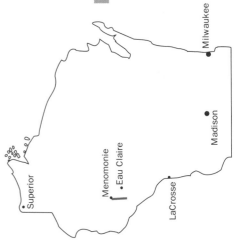

Red Cedar Trail Northern Wisconsin

Menomonie to Chippewa River Trail 14 miles

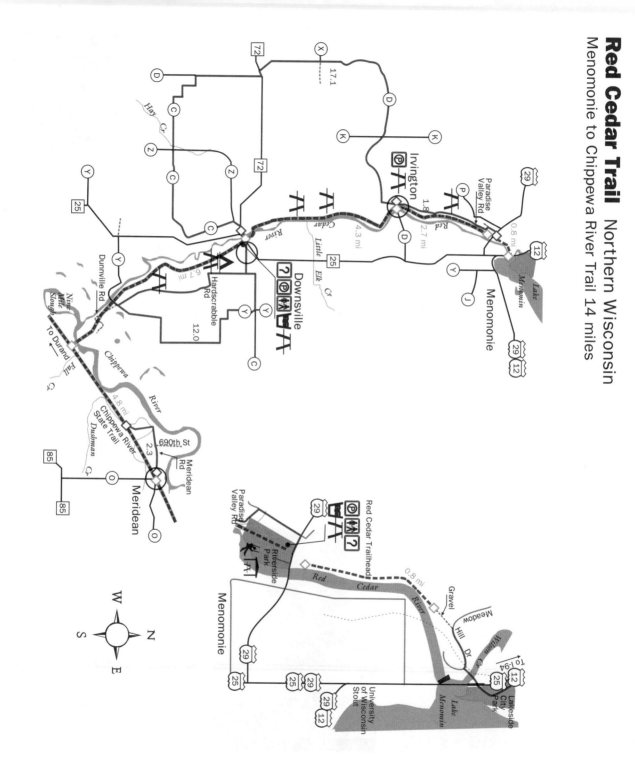

Northern Wisconsin **Red Cedar Trail**

TOURIST INFORMATION

Greater Menomonie Chamber of Commerce
Toll Free (800) 283-1862
Phone (715) 235-9087
Email info@menomoniechamber.org
Web www.menomoniechamber.org

Red Cedar State Trail, DNR,
Menomonie
Phone (715) 232-1242
Web www.dnr.state.wi.us

LODGING

Motels/Resorts

Downsville
The Creamery Restaurant & Inn
P.O. Box 22
Phone (715) 664-8354
Fax (715) 664-8353
Email see website
Web www.creameryrestaurant-inn.com

Menomonie
AmericInn
1915 N Broadway
Toll Free (800) 329-1220
Phone (715) 235-4800
Fax (715) 235-5090
Web www.americinnmenomonie.com

Best Western/Holiday Manor
1815 N Broadway
Toll Free (800) 622-0504
Phone (715) 235-9651
Web www.bestwesternmenomonie.com

Motel 6
2100 Stout Street
Phone (715) 235-6901
Fax (715) 235-8446

Bed and Breakfast

Menomonie
Cedar Trail Guest House
E4761 County Road C
Phone (715) 664-8828

Hansen Heritage House
919-13th Street
Phone (715) 235-0119
Web www.hansenheritagehouse.com

Oaklawn Bed & Breakfast
423 Technology Drive
Toll Free (866) 235-5296
Phone (715) 235-6155
Email info@oaklawnbnb.com
Web www.oaklawnbnb.com

Camping

Menomonie
Twin Springs Campground
Cedar Falls Rd
N 6572 530th Street
Phone (715) 235-9321

BIKE RENTAL

Menomonie
Trail Head Sports
Phone (714) 233-1852
Email trailheadsports@ameritech.net

BIKE REPAIR

Menomonie
Simple Sports
Toll Free (877) 787-5915
Phone (715) 233-3493
Web www.simplesports.us

Trail Head Sports
Phone (715) 233-1852
Email trailheadsports@ameritech.net

FESTIVALS AND EVENTS

Downsville

August

Discover Downsville Days
A celebration of abundance featuring arts and crafts, local food processors and growers, puppet show and other activities for kids, Creamery Restaurant, Fourth Weekend
Phone (715) 664-8355
Web www.creameryrestaurant-inn.com

Menomonie

All Summer

Outdoor Concerts
Ludington Guard Band, oldest community concert band in Wisconsin. Wilson Park Band Shell at 8 pm on Tuesday evenings.
Toll Free (800) 283-1862
Phone (715) 235-9087
Web www.menomoniechamber.org

GROCERIES

Menomonie
Lammer's Foods
(715) 235-2134

Menomonie Market Food Coop
(715) 235-6533

June

Drums Along the Red Cedar
Drum and Bugle competition at the Williams Center, downtown. Check website for details.
Web www.darc.us

August

Dunn County Fair
Animal exhibits, rides, games and special events. Check website for date.
Phone (715) 235-0032
Web www.menomoniechamber.org

Fur Trade Rendezvous
At the Russell J. Rassbach Heritage Museum; Learn about life in a fur trader encampment: black powder shooting, tomahawk throwing, and more. Check website for dates.
Phone (715) 232-8685
Web http://discover-net.net/~dchs

Downsville

Empire in Pine Lumber Museum
Relive the logging camp era of Dunn County's early days. Displays of Knapp, Stout & Company, once the largest white pinery in the world. Open Fri., Sat., Sun., 12–5.
Phone (715) 232-8685
Email dchs@discover-net.net
Web www.discover-net.net/~dchs

Menomonie

Bullfrog Fish Farm
Pole and bait available, hatchery tours, catch cleaned and iced
Phone (715) 664-8775
Email bullfrog@eatmyfish.com
Web www.eatmyfish.com

Farmers Market
Fresh produce, crafts and arts every Saturday and Wednesday from June through October
Toll Free (800) 283-1862
Phone (715) 235-9087
Web www.menomoniechamber.org

Hoffman Hills State Recreation Area
Hilly, wooded recreation area, 60 foot observation tower at top of hill, self-guided nature and hiking trails
Phone (608) 266-2181
Email wiparks@dnr.state.wi.us
Web www.dnr.state.wi.us

Mabel Tainter Theater and Memorial Gallery
Lavishly furnished and restored 1889 theater with exhibit gallery, hand-carved woodwork, bronze cast opera seats and a rare working Steere and Turner tracker pipe organ. Variety of performances.
Toll Free (800) 236-7675
Phone (715) 235-0111
Email mtainter@mabeltainter.com
Web www.mabeltainter.com

Roscoe's Red Cedar Outfitters
Canoe and tube rentals
Phone (715) 235-5431

Russell J. Rassbach Heritage Museum
Chronicles the development of Dunn County through its extensive collection of artifacts and photographs. Open Wed. through Sun., 10–5.
Phone (715) 232-8685
Email dchs@discover-net.net
Web http://discover-net.net/~dchs

Wakanda Waterpark
Outdoor swimming facility, a 230 foot long water slide, interactive water play equipment, sand volleyball

courts, playground equipment, picnic shelters, concession stand
Phone (715) 232-1664
Email menorec@wwt.net
Web www.menomonierecreation.org

Wilson Place Mansion Museum
Museum of local history, including furnishings of lumber baron William Wilson
Toll Free (800) 368-7384
Phone (715) 235-5435

Chippewa River Trail

Vital Information:

Trail Distance: 29 miles

Trail Surface: asphalt

Access Points: Eau Claire, Highway 85 Rest Stop, Caryville, Meridean, Durand

Fees and Passes: Wisconsin State Trail Pass; $3 daily fee or $10 for an annual pass. State Trail passes are good on all Wisconsin State Trails.

Trail Website:
http://www.dnr.state.wi.us

This trail runs from the park-like setting of Eau Claire's city trail through the open farmland of Caryville, into Dunnville Wildlife Area west of Meridean and finishes in Durand. The Red Cedar Trail intersects the Chippewa between Durand and Meridean at an 860 foot railroad trestle across the Chippewa River.

TRAIL HIGHLIGHTS

Blend two trails for a unique look at the Dunnville Wildlife Area and the Chippewa River. Start in Meridean, ride west to the intersection with the Red Cedar Trail, cross the trestle and continue north along the Red Cedar Trail to Downsville. The middle area of the trail passes through wide open farm fields and can get a bit tedious. Consider the road. Beginning at the Highway 85 rest area, the trail winds along the Chippewa River, then crosses near Highway 12 on a beautiful old railroad bridge and follows the north shore past the University of Wisconsin, Eau Claire into Owen Park. The ride through town is quite pleasant with historical markers and great views of the river.

ABOUT THE ROADS

Hilly, twisting and low traffic, the best road routes start from the Highway 85 rest area. If you like hills, these are ideal roads for loops of 12 to 35 miles.

ROAD HIGHLIGHTS

Hwy 85 has traffic, but the shoulder is paved. Mitchell Rd is relatively flat with a beautiful full canopy tree cover.

County F has long, medium rollers, surrounded by a blend of forest and fields. County W is a narrow, snakelike road. It twists and turns, climbs and descends creating scenic views and narrow, intimate trails through the woods. The southern end of County Z repeats the snakelike motions of County W, but passes through a more open landscape. Schuh and Town Hall Roads provide an interesting rolling alternate to the flatlands surrounding the trail between the Highway 85 rest area and Caryville.

HOW TO GET THERE

Eau Claire is 87 miles east of the Twin Cities on Interstate 94 and 87 miles north of LaCrosse on Highway 53. You can avoid going into Eau Claire by taking the Hwy 37/85 exit off Interstate 94. Stay on Highway 85 to the rest area. Caryville, Meridean and Durand can be reached off Hwy 85. If you are from Eau Claire, you can get on the state trail by following the Eau Claire city trail along the Chippewa River through town. See city and trail maps for details.

Chippewa River Trail Northern Wisconsin
Eau Claire to Durand 29 miles

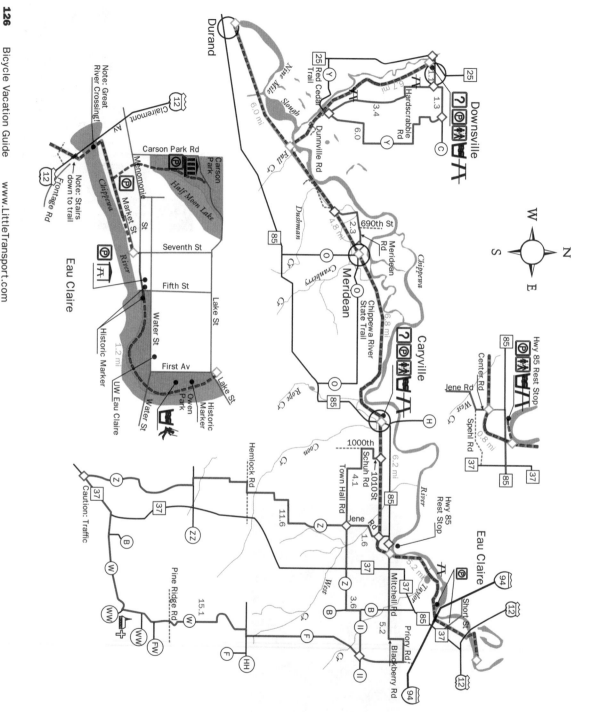

Chippewa River Trail

Northern Wisconsin

TOURIST INFORMATION

Chippewa Valley Convention & Visitors Bureau
Toll Free (888) 523-3866
Phone (715) 831-2345
Fax (715) 831-2340
Email info@chippewavalley.net
Web www.chippewavalley.net

LODGING

Motels/Resorts

Augusta
Woodland Store, Motel & Campground
S5340 State Road 27
Phone (715) 286-2112

Eau Claire
Holiday Inn Campus Area
2703 Craig Road
Phone (715) 835-2211
Web www.holiday-inn.com/eau-campus

The Plaza Hotel & Suites
1202 W. Clairemont Ave
Toll Free (800) 482-7829
Phone (715) 834-3181
Fax (715) 834-2559
Email becky@plazaeauclaire.com
Web www.plazaeauclaire.com

Bed and Breakfast

Eau Claire
Apple Tree Inn Bed & Breakfast
6700 Hwy 53 South
Toll Free (800) 347-9598
Phone (715) 836-9599
Email comments@chippewavalleybb.com
Web www.appletreeinnbb.com

The Atrium
5572 Prill Road
Toll Free (888) 773-0094
Web www.atriumbb.com

Camping

Augusta
Woodland Store, Motel & Campground
S5340 State Road 27
Phone (715) 286-2112

GROCERIES

Eau Claire
Copps Food Center
(715) 834-3993

BIKE RENTAL

Eau Claire
Bike Doctor
Phone (715) 835-4812
Email info@bikedoctor-ec.com
Web www.bikedoctor-ec.com

Riverside Bike & Skate
Phone (715) 835-0088

BIKE REPAIR

Eau Claire
Anybody's Bikeshop
Phone (715) 833-7100

Bike Doctor
Phone (715) 835-4812
Email info@bikedoctor-ec.com
Web www.bikedoctor-ec.com

Eau Claire Bike & Sport
Phone (715) 832-6149

Fitness Factory
Phone (715) 835-1570

Riverside Bike & Skate
Phone (715) 835-0088

FESTIVALS AND EVENTS

Eau Claire

July

Country Jam, USA
Outdoor country music festival with more than thirty top national acts. Side stage entertainment, food and camping, Summer Festival Grounds, Check website for dates.
Toll Free (800) 780-0526
Web www.countryjam.com

August

Festival in the Pines
Arts and crafts, food vendors, games, rides, and family entertainment, Carson Park, Fourth Weekend
Toll Free (888) 611-7463
Phone (715) 552-5504
Web www.festivalinthepines.com

Chippewa River Trail

Northern Wisconsin

Pioneer Days
Flea Market, steamer, games, food stand, tractor pull, crosscut saw competition, parade, Second Weekend
Phone (715) 839-7678

Rendezvous Days
Crafters, games and great food, Third Weekend
Phone (715) 831-2839

USA Amateur Baseball Invitational
college and semi-pro players compete in wood bat baseball tournament at Carson Park. Check website for dates
Toll Free (800) 344-3866
Phone (715) 834-3998
Web www.eauclairecavaliers.org

ALTERNATE ACTIVITIES

Dunnville

Dunnville Wildlife Area
Right on the trail, where the Chippewa and Red Cedar trails intersect.
Toll Free (888) 523-3866
Phone (715) 831-2345
Email info@chippewavalley.net
Web www.dnr.state.wi.us

Eau Claire

Chippewa Valley Museum
Ojibwe Indian culture & frontier heritage, includes Anderson Log House and the one-room Sunnyview School
Phone (715) 834-7871
Fax (715) 834-6624
Email info@cvmuseum.com
Web www.cvmuseum.com

Fanny Hill Victoria Inn & Dinner Theater
Good food and professional dinner theater performances.
Toll Free (800) 292-8026
Phone (715) 836-8184

Fax (715) 836-8180
Email See website
Web www.fannyhill.com

Hank Aaron Statue
Bronze sculpture in Carson Park, Aaron began his playing days for the Eau Claire Bears in 1952
Toll Free (888) 523-3866
Phone (715) 831-2345
Email info@chippewavalley.net
Web www.chippewavalley.net

Paul Bunyan Logging Camp
1900 logging era buildings, including bunkhouse, cook shanty, heavy equipment building, blacksmith shop, and barn, in Carson Park
Phone (715) 835-6200
Fax (715) 835-6293
Email info@paulbunyancamp.org
Web www.paulbunyancamp.org

Riverside Bike & Skate
Canoes, kayaks, paddle and pedal trips on the Eau Claire and Chippewa Rivers
Phone (715) 835-0088

Rude Trude Flyfishing Services
Learn to flyfish for brook, brown and rainbow trout, lessons or guide service. During trout season, May to Sept.
Phone (715) 832-2377
Email rudetrude@pixelclique.net
Web www.rudetrude.com

Ski Sprites Waterski Show
Water ski performances, including bare footing, jumping, pyramids and more, Half Moon Lake, Wednesday and Sunday evenings at 6:30, June through August
Phone (715) 836-9048
Web www.ecol.net/skisprites

Great River Trail

Vital Information:

Trail Distance: 22 miles

Trail Surface: limestone

Access Points: Marshland, Perrot State Park, Trempealeau, Lytles Landing, Midway, Onalaska

Fees and Passes: Wisconsin State Trail Pass; $3 daily fee or $10 for an annual pass. State Trail passes are good on all Wisconsin State Trails.

18 bridges, Mississippi River bottoms and open prairie mark the scenery along this trail. The dam in Onalaska backs up the Mississippi creating scenic Lake Onalaska. Plan your ride to be next to the lake for a stunning sunset. The trail crosses the many branches of the Black River. Sit quietly at the bridges for glimpses of shorebirds, beaver, muskrats, etc. This is a very quiet, remote trail with a lot of diversity. The town of Trempealeau is worth leaving the trail to see. Ask about the outdoor music schedule at the Trempealeau Hotel and stop for a meal. The food is very good.

TRAIL HIGHLIGHTS

The bridge at Lytles Landing passes over the main branch of the Black River and well into the lowlands surrounding the Mississippi River. It's long, low and inviting. For a unique experience spend some time in the Trempealeau National Wildlife Refuge. You may see turkeys on Wildlife Drive, egrets and Great Blue Herons in the marshes, plus pelicans and migratory waterfowl at the observation deck. The surface isn't as solid for bike tires as the trail, but traffic is low and the combination of prairie, wetland and natural history signs makes it worth an extended visit. Pick up a brochure at the parking lot.

ABOUT THE ROADS

Choose your route according to your riding needs. The roads are flat south of Highways 35/54 and hilly north. The flat roads pass through corn fields and open farmland. The hilly roads offer a mix of woodlots, pasture and farmland, some of it from high, scenic vantage

points. Most of the roads in this area are paved and low traffic as long as you stay off the major highways.

ROAD HIGHLIGHTS

The county roads north of Highways 35/54 pass through deep dry valleys called coulees. This kind of riding is addictive. The road slowly rises or falls as long as you are following a creek or small river. Passing from one watershed to another, however, guarantees lots of large hills. For a flatter loop with occasional views of Lake Onalaska, a backwater of the Mississippi, try the roads around Brice Prairie. You can start near Midway and end at Lytles Landing by taking County Roads Z and ZB. Avoid County Road ZN, especially near Midway, because of traffic. The road route through Onalaska follows low traffic, back roads, but isn't especially interesting. It does lead to Rowe Park, a large, well appointed city park, and to the trailhead at the Chamber of Commerce building. A connector from the trailhead leads to the LaCrosse River Trail.

HOW TO GET THERE

Onalaska is just north of LaCrosse in southwestern Wisconsin. Interstate 90 passes along the southern edge of Onalaska. Take Highway 35 north from Interstate 90 to get to the trailhead. See city map. Continue north on Highway 35 to Midway or Trempealeau. From the northwest, cross the Mississippi River on Highway 54 in Winona. Highways 54 and 35 meet in Wisconsin. Watch for Marshland and the Wildlife Refuge sign for parking. Continue along Highway 35 to Trempealeau or Perrot State Park for a better starting point.

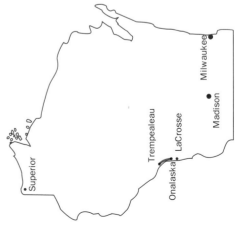

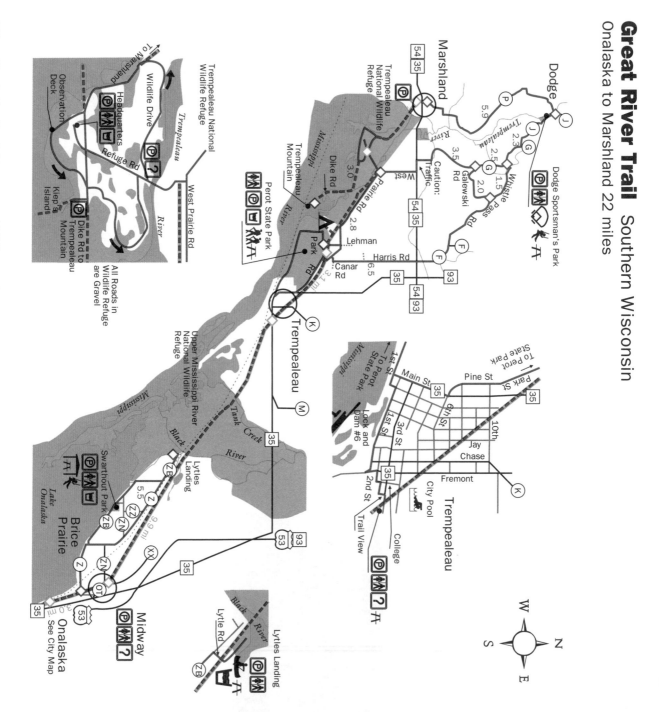

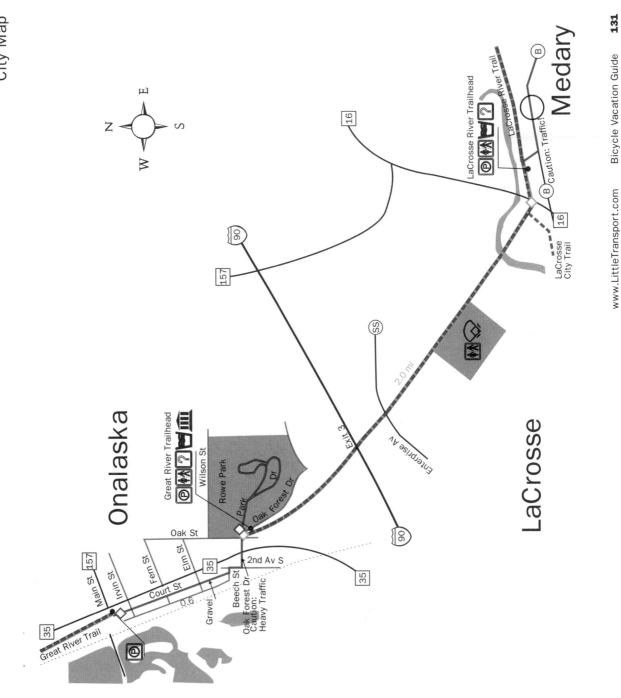

Onalaska

LaCrosse

Medary

Great River Trail Southern Wisconsin

TOURIST INFORMATION

Onalaska Center for Commerce and Tourism
Toll Free (800) 873-1901
Phone (608) 781-9570
Fax (608) 781-9572
Email info@discoveronalaska.com
Web www.discoveronalaska.com

Perrot State Park and Great River Trail
Phone (608) 534-6409
Web www.dnr.state.wi.us

Trempealeau Chamber of Commerce
Phone (608) 534-6780
Email chamber@trempealeau.net
Web http://www.trempealeau.net

LODGING

Motels/Resorts

Onalaska
Baymont Inns & Suites
Toll Free (877) 392-7950
Phone (608) 783-7191

Comfort Inn
1223 Crossing Meadows Dr
Toll Free (800) 228-5150
Phone (608) 781-7500

Hampton Inn
Toll Free (800) 426-7866
Phone (608) 779-5000

Holiday Inn Express
Toll Free (800) 411-3712
Phone (608) 783-6555

Lake Motel
Phone (608) 783-3348

Micro Tel Inn
Toll Free (888) 818-2359
Phone (608) 783-0833

Onalaska Inn
Hwy 35
Toll Free (888) 359-2619
Phone (608) 783-2270

Shadow Run Lodge
710 2nd Ave. N
Toll Free (800) 657-4749
Phone (608) 783-0020

Trempealeau
Inn on the River
First and Main St
PO Box 335
Phone (608) 534-7784
Email innontheriver@triwest.net
Web www.ExploreWisconsin.com/innon-theriver

The Historic Trempealeau Hotel
150 Main Street
Phone (608) 534-6898
Web www.trempealeauhotel.com

Bed and Breakfast

Onalaska
Rainbow Ridge Farms and B & B
W 5732 Hauser Rd.
Phone (608) 783-8181
Web www.rainbowridgefarms.com

The Lumber Baron Inn Bed & Breakfast
421 2nd Ave N
Phone (608) 781-8938

Trempealeau
Lucas House Bed & Breakfast
24616 2nd Street
Phone (608) 534-6665
Web www.trempealeau.net/lucas

Camping

LaCrosse
Goose Island Campground
W6488 Cty Rd Gl
Phone (608) 788-7018
Fax (608) 788-0612
Email campthegoose@centurytel.net

Trempealeau
Perrot State Park
Rt1, Box 407
Toll Free (888) 947-2757
Phone (608) 534-6409
Web www.wiparks.net

GROCERIES

Onalaska
Kwik Trip Stores
(608) 779-9364

Trempealeau
Budget Mart
(608) 534-6554

Southern Wisconsin **Great River Trail**

BIKE RENTAL

La Crosse
Smith's Cycling & Fitness
Phone (608) 779-0510
Web www.smithsbikes.com

Trempealeau
The Historic Trempealeau Hotel
Phone (608) 534-6898
Web www.trempealeauhotel.com

BIKE REPAIR

La Crosse
Smith Cycle & Fitness
Phone (608) 779-0510
Web www.smithsbike.com

FESTIVALS AND EVENTS

Onalaska

May
Sunfish Days
Kids' fishing derby, craft fair, volleyball and softball tourneys, carnival rides, petting zoo, parade, live music, beer garden, food stands, Omni Center at Van Riper Park. Check website for details.
Toll Free (800) 873-1901
Phone (608) 781-9570
Web www.discoveronalaska.com

July
Salute to the Fourth
Kids' games, craft and food booths, beer tent, evening fireworks in conjunction with LaCrosse Symphony Orchestra, always July 1st, regardless of day of the week
Toll Free (800) 873-1901
Phone (608) 781-9570
Web www.discoveronalaska.com

September
Fall 15 Great River Walk
Four, nine, or 15 mile fitness walk along the Great River Trail from Onalaska to Trempealeau, shuttles and snacks on the trail, dinner, prizes and entertainment in Trempealeau, advance registration required, Saturday after Labor Day
Toll Free (800) 873-1901
Phone (608) 781-9570
Web www.discoveronalaska.com

Oktoberfest
At the La Crosse Oktoberfest grounds, German Fall Festival: food, music entertainment, carnival, crafts, sporting events, torchlight parade. Check website for dates.
Toll Free (800) 873-1901
Phone (608) 782-3378
Web www.discoveronalaska.com

Trempealeau
All Summer
Stars under the Stars
Outdoor summer concert series featuring national acts at the historic Trempealeau Hotel concert grounds.
Phone (608) 534-6898
Web www.trempealeauhotel.com

May

Blues Bash

Nationally and internationally famous blues bands from early afternoon through the evening at the Trempealeau Hotel concert grounds. Check website for date.
Phone (608) 534-6898
Web www.trempealeauhotel.com

Reggae Sunsplash

Jamaican style music, food and crafts from early afternoon through the evening, Trempealeau Hotel concert grounds. Check website for details.
Phone (608) 534-6898
Web www.trempealeauhotel.com

Trempealeau Hipbreaker Bike Tour

10, 23 and 43 mile tours, along the Mississippi River and Perrot State Park. Check website for details and date.
Web www.trempealeau.net

July

Catfish Days

Bike tour and race, art and craft fair, flea market, fishing tournament, kids' games and parade, live music, dancing, carnival, beer tent, parade on Sunday and fireworks in the evening.

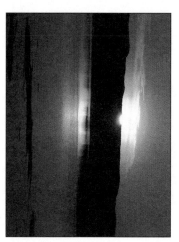

First weekend following the 4th
Phone (608) 543-6780
Web http://www.trempealeau.net/

Onalaska

Bird Watching

Bird watching along the Mississippi River during spring and fall migration at Highway 35 North overlooking Lake Onalaska, two observation points with interpretive signs
Phone (608) 783-8405
Web http://wisconsinaudubon.com

Lake Onalaska

Fishing, canoeing, kayaking, bird-watching, sailboarding
Phone (507) 452-4232
Email uppermississippiriver@fws.gov
Web http://midwest.fws.gov/
UpperMississippiRiver/

Trempealeau

Al's Canoe Rental and Shuttle Service

Canoes available for canoeing the Trempealeau River, Black River, Long Lake Canoe Trail, Trempealeau Bay or the Wildlife Refuge Pools.
Phone (608) 534-5046

Lock and Dam #6

Watch boats and barges go through the locks on the Mississippi River. Near Trempealeau.
Phone (608) 534-6424
Web www.recreation.gov

Long Lake Canoe Trail

Canoe through the Upper Mississippi River National Wildlife and Fish Refuge, travel 4.5 miles in about 2 hours through sloughs and islands that are a haven for wildlife.

Phone (608) 783-8405
Email uppermississippiriver@fws.gov
Web http://midwest.fws.gov/LaCrosse/

Perrot State Park

1,400 acres nestled among bluffs where the Trempealeau and Mississippi rivers meet. Scenic hikes to the top of the bluffs, including Brady's Bluff Prairie, a goat prairie on the bluff rising 460 feet above the Mississippi River
Phone (608) 534-6409

Trempealeau Hotel

Historic Trempealeau Hotel retains its classic 1888 charm, while still offering modern style. On the banks of the Mississippi: bike and canoe rentals
Phone (608) 534-6898
Web www.trempealeauhotel.com

Trempealeau National Wildlife Refuge

View a variety of animal and plant life in wetland, sand prairie and bottomland hardwood forest habitats. Roads are gravel but bikeable. Some go deep into the marshlands of the Mississippi River
Phone (608) 539-2311
Email uppermississippiriver@fws.gov
Web http://midwest.fws.gov/
UpperMississippiRiver

LaCrosse River Trail

Vital Information:

Trail Distance: 21 miles

Trail Surface: limestone

Access Points: Onalaska, Medary, West Salem, Bangor, Rockland, Sparta

Fees and Passes: Wisconsin State Trail Pass; $3 daily fee or $10 for an annual pass. State Trail passes are good on all Wisconsin State Trails.

Trail Website: www.lacrosserivertrail.org

ABOUT THE TRAIL

This trail has a rap for not being very scenic and there is some justification for it, but taken selectively, it has some real charms. The connecting road routes are very nice, so it is possible to tie together the better parts of the trail with scenic roads to create some very enjoyable rides. For long distance riders, the trail links the Great River Trail on the west with the Elroy-Sparta Trail to the east. It is possible to travel over 100 miles with only one minor break in the trail system.

TRAIL HIGHLIGHTS

Between Medary and West Salem the trail passes through the vast floodplain of the LaCrosse River. Lots of marshland, wet prairie and backwaters offer good bird and wildlife watching if you ride early morning or near sunset. Day time is good for viewing a wide variety of wetland grasses and flowers. Veteran's Memorial Park in West Salem is a unique memorial to local veterans who died in US wars. The Dutch Creek Swimming hole, right off the trail in Bangor City Park, offers a refreshing dip in a shaded creek. Great for cooling off on a hot summer day. The native prairie east of Rockland has some nice wildflowers, but is a little disappointing as a prairie.

ABOUT THE ROADS

Take your pick. You get a little of everything from the nearly flat roads between Bangor and Sparta to the extremely long climb over Mindoro Pass. This is primarily dairy country where contour plowed fields of corn and alfalfa form a patchwork of zig zag fields mixed with pastures and woodlots. Monroe County has a cold weather theme between the county line and Sparta. Check out the road names as you ride them or cross them.

ROAD HIGHLIGHTS

The Mindoro loop climbs to high scenic vistas and rural panoramic views. The climbs are long and challenging. The descents are exciting. Mindoro is charming. The sidewalk rises six feet above the street to create a porch-like setting with roof, railings and rest benches. If the bank is open, stop in for a look at the collection of photos showing how Mindoro Pass was cut by hand near the turn of the century. While the Mindoro Loop spends its time on the ridge, the southern loop, between Medary and Bangor, follows the creeks and valleys. From west to east, the valley walls slowly close in until the road turns and begins a long steep climb, followed by a fast descent. East of Bangor, the road routes offer a diverse, nearly flat alternate to the trail. Take the trail one way and the roads on the way back. From Hammer Road to Sparta, take the trail because Iberia carries some traffic, including trucks.

HOW TO GET THERE

Interstate 90 parallels the trail from LaCrosse to Sparta. All trail towns are easily accessible from the Interstate. To get to Medary, take the Highway 16 exit off Interstate 90, go south to County Road B, and east on B to the trailhead.

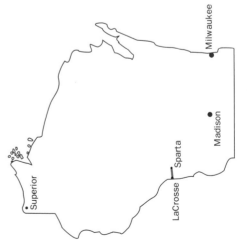

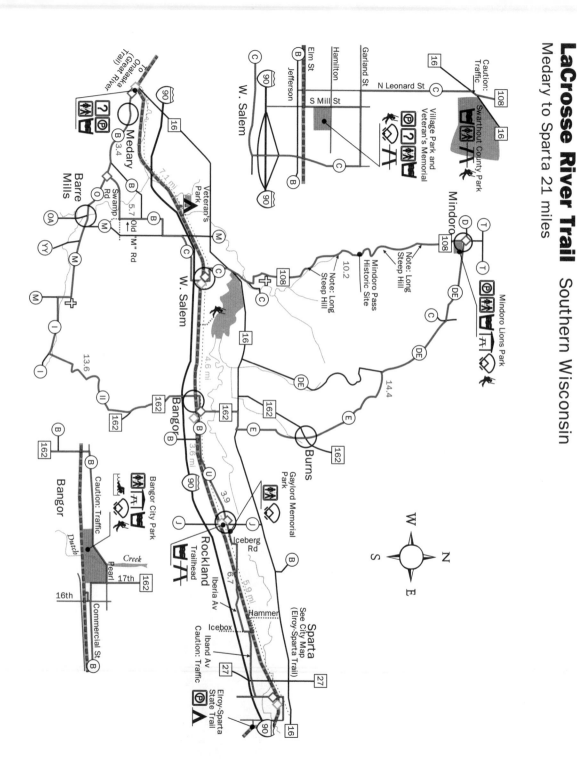

W. Salem

Mindoro

Mindoro Lions Park

Note: Long Steep Hill

Note: Long Steep Hill

Mindoro Pass Historic Site

10.2

14.4

Caution: Traffic

Swarthout County Park

Village Park and Veteran's Memorial

N Leonard St

Garland St

Hamilton

Elm St

Jefferson

S Mill St

Medary

3.4

7.1 mi

Veteran's Park

Barre Mills

Swamp Rd

Old "M" Rd

5.7

W. Salem

4.6 mi

13.6

Bangor

3.6 mi

162

Burns

Gaylord Memorial Park

E

Rockland Trailhead

Iceberg Rd

Iberia Av

3.9

6.7

5.9 mi

Hammen

Icebox

Iband Av

Caution: Traffic

Bangor City Park

Caution: Traffic

Bangor

Dutch Creek

Pearl

17th

16th

Commercial St

Sparta

See City Map (Elroy-Sparta Trail)

Elroy-Sparta State Trail

To Onalaska (Great River Trail)

N
W   E
S

LaCrosse River Trail

Southern Wisconsin

TOURIST INFORMATION

Greater LaCrosse Area Chamber of Commerce
Toll Free (800) 889-0539
Phone (608) 784-4880
Fax (608) 784-4919
Email lse_chamber@centuryinter.net
Web www.lacrossechamber.com

LaCrosse Area Convention and Visitors Bureau
Toll Free (800) 658-9424
Phone (608) 782-2366
Web www.explorelacrosse.com

LaCrosse River State Trail
Toll Free (888) 540-8434
Phone (608) 269-4123
Fax (608) 269-3350
Email spartachamber@centurytel.net
Web www.LaCrosseRiverStateTrail.org

Onalaska Center for Commerce and Tourism
Toll Free (800) 873-1901
Phone (608) 781-9570
Email info@discoveronalaska.com
Web www.discoveronalaska.com

Sparta Chamber of Commerce
Toll Free (800) 354-2453
Phone (608) 269-4123
Fax (608) 269-3350

Email spartachamber@centurytel.net
Web www.spartachamber.org

Sparta Convention and Visitors Bureau
Toll Free (800) 354-2453
Phone (608) 269-2453
Web www.spartawisconsin.org

Village of West Salem
Phone (608) 786-1858
Fax (608) 786-1988
Email info@westsalemwi.com
Web www.westsalemwi.com

Wildcat Mountain State Park
Phone (608) 337-4775
Web www.dnr.state.wi.us

Email chateaulax@aol.com
Web www.chateaulacrosse.com

Four Gables Inn
W 5648 Hwy 14-61
Phone (608) 788-7958

Onalaska
See Great River Trail

Sparta
See Elroy-Sparta Trail

Camping

Onalaska
See Great River Trail

Sparta
See Elroy-Sparta Trail

Stoddard
Goose Island Campground
W6488 County Rd GI
Phone (608) 788-7018

West Salem
Veterans Memorial Campground
N4668 CTH VP
Phone (608) 786-4011

LODGING

Motels/Resorts

Onalaska
See Great River Trail

Sparta
See Elroy-Sparta Trail

Bed and Breakfast

La Crosse
Chateau La Crosse
410 Cass Street
Toll Free (800) 442-7969
Phone (608) 796-1090
Fax (608) 796-0700

GROCERIES

Bangor
Hansen's IGA
(608) 486-2626

West Salem
Cenex Convenience Store
(608) 786-1108

LaCrosse River Trail

Southern Wisconsin

BIKE RENTAL

LaCrosse
Smith's Cycling & Fitness
Phone (608) 779-0510
Web www.smithsbikes.com

Buzz's Bicycle Shop
Phone (608) 785-2737

Sparta
See Elroy Sparta Trail

BIKE REPAIR

LaCrosse
Smith's Cycling & Fitness
Phone (608) 779-0510
Web www.smithsbikes.com

Bikes Limited
Phone (608) 785-2326

Buzz's Bikes
Phone (608) 785-2737

Valley Ski & Bike
Phone (608) 782-5500

Sparta
See Elroy-Sparta Trail

FESTIVALS AND EVENTS

Onalaska
See Great River Trail

Sparta
See Elroy-Sparta Trail

West Salem

June
June Dairy Days
Kickoff breakfast, parade at noon on
Saturday, carnival, softball games, live
music, clowns, magicians, food, dairy
tents, bingo, petting barn, stagecoach
rides. Village Park: Check website for
dates.

Phone (608) 786-1858
Web www.westsalemwi.com

Le Coulee Classique Bike Ride
Organized ride with the option of 35 or
60 miles, sag wagon and rest stops,
part of June Dairy Days, First
Weekend
Phone (608) 779-5229

July
LaCrosse Interstate Fair
Rural fair, with animals, 4-H projects,
carnival and food booths. Call for dates.
Phone (608) 786-0428

ALTERNATE ACTIVITIES

Bangor
Bangor City Park
Old fashioned swimming hole in Dutch
Creek, visible from the trail
Phone (608) 486-4084

Onalaska
See Great River Trail

Rockland
Restored Prairie
Along the trail.
Phone (608) 486-4037

Sparta
See Elroy-Sparta Trail

Village of Ontario
Wildcat Mountain State Park
Scenic vistas and great hiking trails
Phone (608) 337-4775
Web www.dnr.state.wi.us

West Salem
Historic West Salem
Home of Hamlin Garland, Pulitzer Prize
winning author, also two octagon
homes, Thomas Leonard's colonial
style home, check out Veterans'
Memorial Park
Email info@westsalemwi.com
Web www.westsalemwi.com

Wolfway Farm
One of Wisconsin's Century Farms,
registered Holsteins are milked twice
daily, reservations required.
Phone (608) 486-2686

Elroy-Sparta Trail

Vital Information:

Trail Distance: 32 miles

Trail Surface: limestone

Access Points: Sparta, Norwalk, Wilton, Kendall, Elroy

Fees and Passes: Wisconsin State Trail Pass; $3 daily fee or $10 for an annual pass. State Trail passes are good on all Wisconsin State Trails.

Trail Website: www.elroy-sparta-trail.org

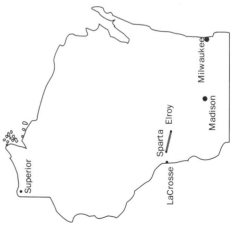

ABOUT THE TRAIL

Developed in 1967, this is the grand-daddy of them all. It shows in the mature trees, full canopy and well maintained trail surface. Bicycling is the main tourism attraction here so you'll have plenty of companionship. The trail rises and drops very slowly as it passes through hilly, scenic, driftless area. Explore the three tunnels, spend an evening in one of the small trail towns and enjoy the camaraderie of riding with cyclists from around the nation. Three major bike trails converge at Elroy Commons in Elroy, creating a hub of bicycle activity. See city maps for details. Weekends and holidays are extremely busy.

TRAIL HIGHLIGHTS

The tunnels are unique, the lead up to the entrances rounds out the experience. The trail rises slowly and passes through deep road cuts near the tunnel entrances, creating a cool, damp micro-environment. Bring flashlights for the tunnels and walk your bike. Water runs along both sides of the trail in the three-quarter mile long Tunnel #3 and falling water splashes loudly near the center. You'll get dripped on lightly in the tunnel. Note the cool breeze flowing out of the lower, western end.

ABOUT THE ROADS

First timers come for the trail. Repeat visitors explore the roads. Expect grinding climbs, hair-raising descents, horse drawn Amish buggies, virtually no traffic, and pastoral views that belong in picture books. The roads will give you the best sense of this hilly, scenic country. Traffic is minimal and the surfaces range from smooth to pebbly.

ROAD HIGHLIGHTS

The town roads between Kendall and Norwalk offer the most challenging climbs and descents near the trail. On one descent, from east to west, we hit 52 miles per hour. County Road T, south of Norwalk, follows a creek bed and stays flat. County Road F branches off and remains relatively flat for several miles, then climbs long and hard to become rolling ridgetop. Check out the church and convent in St. Mary's, then return to Norwalk via County U. Payback comes as U nears Norwalk. 16th Avenue, near Tunnel #3, passes over the tunnel and appears to run right along the top at one point. No markings along here, so you will have to imagine the folks walking in the dark beneath you.

HOW TO GET THERE

Sparta is approximately 25 miles east of LaCrosse on Interstate 94. Take the Highway 27 exit. Go north to Avon Road and follow the city map to the LaCrosse River Trailhead. To go directly to the Elroy-Sparta Trailhead, or to the trail towns, take the Highway 16 exit off Interstate 94. Go west on Highway 16 (toward Sparta) and turn south on Highway 71. To get to Elroy, take I-90/94 to Exit 61 for New Lisbon. Take Hwy 80 south 13 miles to Elroy.

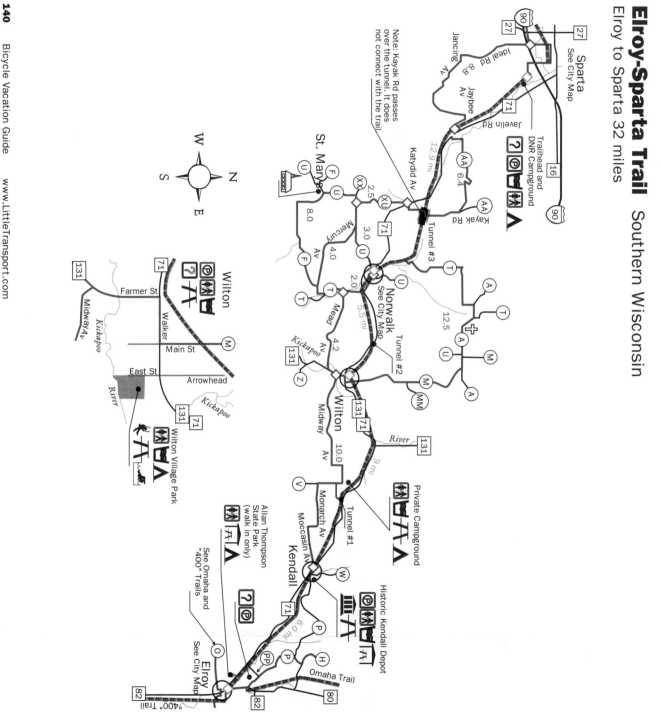

Elroy-Sparta Trail   Southern Wisconsin

Elroy to Sparta 32 miles

Note: Kayak Rd passes over the tunnel. It does not connect with the trail

Sparta
See City Map

Trailhead and DNR Campground

Ideal Rd   8.8

Jancing Av

Jaybee Av

Javelin Rd

12.9 mi

Katydid Av

AA   6.4

Kayak Rd

AA

Tunnel #3

Mercury Av

St. Marys

Norwalk
See City Map

Tunnel #2

12.5

Mead Av

Kickapoo Av

Wilton

Wilton
See City Map

131

Farmer St

Walker

Main St

East St

Arrowhead

Kickapoo

River

Midway Av

Kickapoo   River

Midway Av

Private Campground

Tunnel #1

Moccasin Av

Monarch Av

9 mi

10.0

Kendall

Allan Thompson State Park (walk in only)

Historic Kendall Depot

See Omaha and "400" Trails

Omaha Trail

Elroy
See City Map

"400" Trail

N W E S

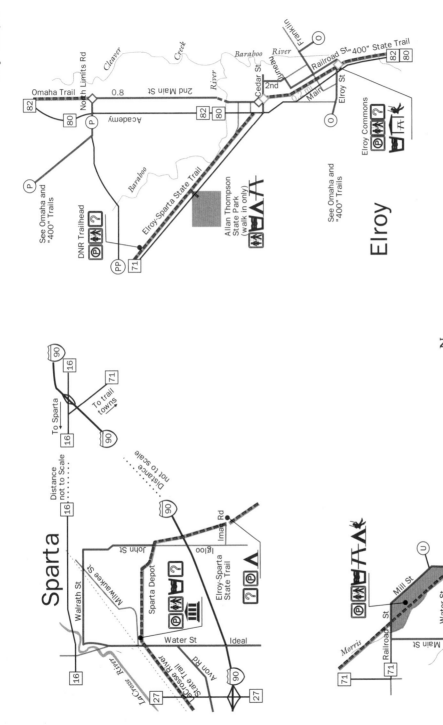

Elroy-Sparta Trail   Southern Wisconsin

WELCOME TO SPARTA, WISCONSIN

TOURIST INFORMATION

Elroy Commons Information Center
Toll Free (888) 606-2453
Phone (608) 462-2410
Email elroywi@mwt.net
Web www.elroywi.com

Kendall Depot
Phone (608) 463-7109
Web www.elroy-sparta-trail.com

Sparta Area Chamber of Commerce
Toll Free (800) 354-2453
Phone (608) 269-4123
Email spartachamber@centurytel.net
Web www.spartachamber.org

Village of Norwalk
Phone (608) 823-7760
Email villageofnorwalk@centurytel.net

Village of Ontario
Phone (608) 337-4381

Village of Wilton
Phone (608) 435-6666
Email villageofwilton@centurytel.net

LODGING

Motels/Resorts

Elroy
Valley Inn Motel
1/2 mile South on Hwy 80 & 82
Phone (608) 462-4330
Web www.valleyinnelroy.com

Kendall
Country Livin' Motel & Guest Apt.
Hwy 71
Phone (608) 463-7135

Sparta
Best Nights Inn
303 West Wisconsin Street
Toll Free (800) 201-0234
Phone (608) 269-3066
Web www.bestnightsinn.com

Country Inn By Carlson
737 Avon Rd
Toll Free (800) 456-4000
Phone (608) 269-3110

Justin Trails Resort
7452 Kathyrn Ave
Toll Free (800) 488-4521
Phone (608) 269-4522
Email info@justintrails.com
Web www.justintrails.com

Spartan Motel
1900 W. Wisconsin St
Phone (608) 269-2770

Super 8 Motel
716 Avon Road
Toll Free (800) 800-8000
Phone (608) 269-8489
Web www.super8.com

Wilton
Mid-Trail Motel
P.O. Box 296
Hwy 71
Phone (608) 435-6685

Bed and Breakfast

Elroy
Eastview
33620 Cty P
Phone (608) 463-7564

Waarvik's Century Farm
N 4621 County Road H
Phone (608) 462-8595
Email waarvik@hotmail.com
Web www.waarvikcenturyfarm.com

Kendall
Cabin at Trails End
23009 Knollwood Rd
Phone (608) 427-3877
Email cabin@mwt.net
Web www.mwt.net/~cabin

Sparta
Cranberry Country B&B
114 Montgomery St
Toll Free (888) 208-4354
Phone (608) 366-1000
Email cranberry@elroynet.com
Web www.cranberrycountrybedand-
breakfast.com

Southern Wisconsin **Elroy-Sparta Trail**

LODGING cont'd

Franklin Victorian Bed and Breakfast
220 East Franklin Street
Toll Free (888) 594-3822
Phone (608) 366-1427
Email see website
Web www.franklinvictorianbb.com

Justin Trails Resort
7452 Kathyrn Ave
Toll Free (800) 488-4521
Phone (608) 269-4522
Email info@justintrails.com
Web www.justintrails.com

Wilton

Dorset Ridge Guest House
22259 King Road
Phone (608) 463-7375

Camping

Elroy

E.O. Schultz Park
City Park in Elroy
Toll Free (888) 606-2453
Phone (608) 462-2410
Web www.elroywi.com

Primitive DNR Campground
Phone (608) 337-4775

LaFarge

Kickapoo Valley Reserve
S 3661 State Hwy 131
Phone (608) 625-2960
Web http://kvr.state.wi.us

Norwalk

Village Park
102 Mill St
Phone (608) 823-7760

Ontario

Brush Creek Campground
S 190 Opal Rd Off Hwy 33
Phone (608) 337-4344

Wildcat Mountain State Park
PO Box 99
Phone (608) 337-4775
Web www.dnr.state.wi.us

Sparta

Leon Valley Campground
9050 Jancing Ave
Phone (608) 269-6400
Email leonvalley@centurytel.net
Web www.campleonvalley.com

Primitive DNR
Trailhead
Web www.dnr.state.wi.us

Wilton

Tunnel Trail Campground
26983 State Hwy 71
Phone (608) 435-6829
Email tunneltrail@elroynet.com
Web http://www.tunneltrail.com

Wilton Village Campground
400 East St
Phone (608) 435-6666

Sparta

Ray's Supermarket
(608) 269-3135

Wilton

Main Street Market
(608) 435-6517

Wilton Fasttrip
(608) 435-6977

BIKE RENTAL

Elroy

Elroy Commons
Toll Free (888) 606-2453
Phone (608) 462-2410
Email elroywi@mwt.net
Web www.elroywi.com

The Bike Hut
Phone (608) 462-5001

Kendall

Kendall Depot
Phone (608) 463-7109
Email kdepot@mwt.net
Web www.elroy-sparta-trail.org

Sparta

Out Spokin' Adventures
Toll Free (800) 493-2453
Phone (608) 269-6087
Email outspokin@centurytel.net
Web www.outspokinadventures.com

GROCERIES

Norwalk

Lehner's Market
(608) 823-7613

BIKE RENTAL cont'd

Speed's Bicycle
Phone (608) 269-2315
Web www.speedsbike.com

Wilton
Tunnel Trail Campground
Phone (608) 435-6829

BIKE REPAIR

Elroy
The Bike Hut
Phone (608) 462-5001

Sparta
Speed's Bicycle
Phone (608) 269-2315
Fax (608) 269-3852

BIKE SHUTTLE

Sparta
Out Spokin' Avdentures
Toll Free (800) 493-2453
Phone (608) 269-6087
Web www.outspokinadventures.com

FESTIVALS AND EVENTS

Elroy
June
Elroy Fair
Carnival, horse pull, livestock judging, tractor pull, demolition derby, 4-H exhibits, music, food. Last Weekend
Toll Free (888) 606-2453
Web www.elroywi.com

Kendall
September
Labor Day Celebration
Volleyball, parade, tractor pull, chicken BBQ, pancake breakfast.
Phone (608) 463-7124

Norwalk
June
Lions Softball Tournament
Last Weekend
Phone (608) 823-7760

August
Black Squirrel Fest
BBQ chicken, softball, tractor pull, pie & ice-cream tent, DJ Saturday night, pancake breakfast on Sunday, Second Weekend
Phone (608) 823-7760

Sparta
June
Butterfest
Carnival, live entertainment, magic shows, arts and crafts exhibits, music, food booths, quilt show, parade, Second Weekend
Toll Free (800) 354-2453

Phone (608) 269-4123
Web www.spartachamber.org

August
Coulee Classic ("Bike Me") Tour
Fully supported, 6-day, 5-night tour of Wisconsin's Coulee Region. 35 - 60 miles daily. Check website for dates.
Toll Free (800) 354-2453
Phone (414) 671-4560
Web www.wisconsinbicycletours.com

Monroe County Bike Challenge
Monroe County Challenge Bike Race, citizens and WISSPORT sanctioned race through Monroe County, 45 miles, bike rodeo, live music, and kids' events, Memorial Park, Second Weekend
Toll Free (800) 947-3564
Phone (608) 269-4123

FESTIVALS AND EVENTS cont'd

Wilton

All Summer

Pancake breakfast
Sonsored by the Lions Club each
Sunday, Memorial Day through Labor
Day, Wilton Village Park
Phone (608) 435-6666

August

Wilton Wood Turtle Days
Fireworks, softball, volleyball, parade,
arts & crafts show, First Sunday
Phone (608) 435-6666

ALTERNATE ACTIVITIES

Sparta

Cabin on the Rock
Located on a 365 acre, four generation, working dairy farm, Holstein
cows, calves, and horseback riding
atop Redrock Ridge, cabin overlooks
the farm including 200 acres of woodlands with plenty of hiking trails, 5
miles to Elroy-Sparta bike trail
Phone (608) 823-7865

Deke Slayton Memorial Space &
Bicycle Museum
Deke Slayton, one of America's origi-
nal astronauts was born in the Sparta
area and raised in Monroe County.
Exhibits from Mercury, Gemini, Apollo
and Space Shuttle missions, also
includes the history of bicycles
Toll Free (888) 200-5302
Phone (608) 269-0033
Email dekeslayton@centurytel.net
Web www.spartan.org

Down A Country Road
Take a tour of the Amish community
and get a glimpse of this unique way
of life, then browse the Amish gift
shop, Highway 33 off Highway 27
Phone (608) 654-5318
Email downacountryroad@yahoo.com
Web downacountryroadamish.com

M&M Ranch
Exotic animal ranch with African
Pygmy hedgehogs, talking parrots,
potbellied pigs, toucans, ferrets,
Scottish Highland cattle, minature
horses & donkeys,
Phone (608) 486-2709
Fax (608) 486-4052
Email m1m2ranch@aol.com
Web www.centuryinter.net/mmranch

Monroe County Local History Museum
& Research Room
The story of Monroe County and its
pioneer history through photographs
and memorabilia, genealogical source
materials including census records,
church, cemetery and school
Phone (608) 269-8680
Email MCLHR@centurytel.net
Web www.spartan.org/historyroom

Out Spokin' Adventures
Kayaks, rentals, with shuttle
Toll Free (800) 493-2453
Phone (608) 269-6087
Email outspokin@centuryinter.net
Web www.outspokinadventures.com

Paul and Matilda Wegner Grotto
Locally known as 'The Glass Church',
an example of grassroots art, For
more information contact the Local
History Room at 200 West Main St,
Sparta
Phone (608) 269-8680
Email MCLHR@centurytel.net

Drifty's Canoe Rental
Canoe rental on the Kickapoo River
Phone (608) 337-4288

Kickapoo Paddle Inn
Canoe rental on the Kickapoo River
Toll Free (800) 947-3603
Phone (608) 337-4726

Wildcat Mountain State Park
Beautiful scenery, nature trails and
camping
Phone (608) 337-4775
Web www.dnr.state.wi.us

Circle "S" Trail Rides
Horseback rides
Phone (608) 435-6975

Omaha and "400" Trails

Vital Information:

Trail Distance: 34 miles

Trail Surface: limestone

Access Points: Omaha-Camp Douglas, Hustler, Elroy, "400"-Elroy, Union Center, Wonewoc, La Valle, Reedsburg

Fees and Passes: 400 Trail:Wisconsin State Trail Pass; $3 daily fee or $10 for an annual pass. State Trail passes are good on all Wisconsin State Trails. Omaha Trail: Daily pass $1.00

Trail Website: www.400statetrail.org

ABOUT THE TRAIL

The Omaha Trail is a paved county trail from Camp Douglas to Elroy. Good for a quick break when traveling the Interstate between the Twin Cities and Milwaukee or Chicago. The "400" Trail more or less follows the Baraboo River and passes through numerous wetlands. Early morning hours are best for wildlife viewing. Lift your eyes away from the trail during the day and take in the bluffs and mounds in the distance. Small towns with scenic parks dot the trail. Both trails meet at the Elroy-Sparta Trail in Elroy creating a lot of opportunities for the repeat or long term visitor.

TRAIL HIGHLIGHTS

The southern end of the Omaha Trail passes through some steep walled valleys as it climbs to the tunnel south of Hustler. Pass through the 875 foot tunnel, then take a break at the rest stop with modern bathrooms and a hand pump for water. The trail follows another small valley before the land levels out near Hustler.

Hemlock Park is a pretty little park across a small lake from the 400 Trail. Take McKinney Road to the park sign and drop down a steep hill to the water's edge. The first two miles from the Reedsburg Depot parallel an active rail line. The trail gets better after the active line branches off. Legion Park offers a pleasant break half a mile from the trail in Wonewoc. The ball diamond in Legion Park is the most romantic, and impractical, playing field I've ever seen.

ABOUT THE ROADS

The roads in this area go through the heart of the Driftless Area. If you don't mind lots of hills, these roads are a delight because of their low traffic and rural panoramas. Asphalt surfaces vary from smooth to patchy or pebbly.

ROAD HIGHLIGHTS

County Road H from Camp Douglas to the tunnel on the Omaha Trail is reasonably flat. It offers a good return route after going one way on the trail. The southern end of Tunnel Road is scenic rolling and offers some great views of the trail. The east and west routes between Elroy and Wonewoc are prime roads if you don't mind hills. Stop at Wonewoc Park and refill your water bottle at the artesian well. Dutch Hollow Road has some traffic on weekends and holidays because of the lake cabins around Dutch Hollow Lake. Same story with County Road V between the trail and Reedsburg. Worth riding if you are comfortable with some traffic.

HOW TO GET THERE

Camp Douglas is on Interstates 90/94 about 10 miles south of the intersection of the two Highways near Tomah. To get to Elroy, stay on the Interstate to Mauston, then take Highway 82 west. To get to Reedsburg, take Interstate 90/94 to Lake Delton, then Highway 23 south to Reedsburg. The Omaha and 400 Trails meet in Elroy, the eastern terminus of the Elroy-Sparta Trail. For more information about getting to the Elroy-Sparta Trail, see previous chapter.

Southern Wisconsin **Omaha Trail**
Camp Douglas to Reedsburg 12 miles

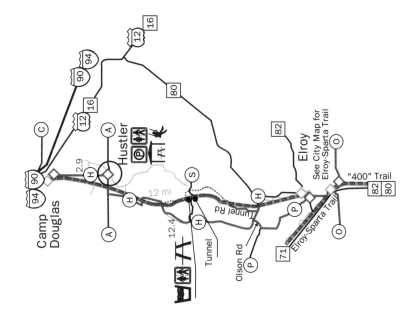

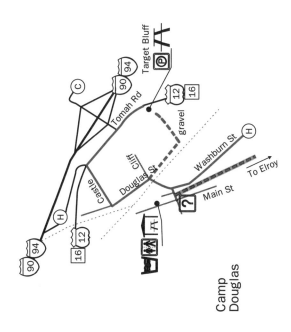

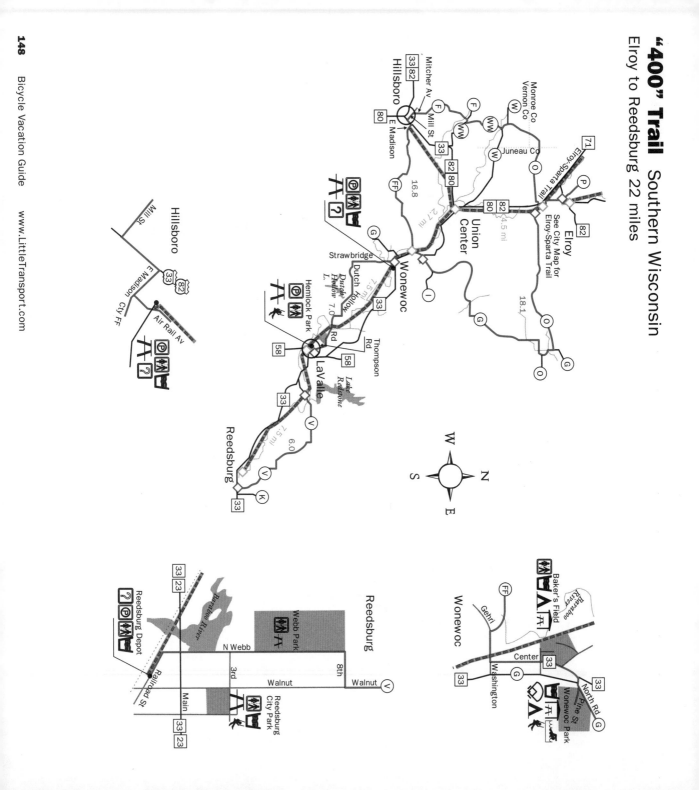

"400" Trail
Southern Wisconsin
Elroy to Reedsburg 22 miles

Southern Wisconsin Omaha and "400" Trails

TOURIST INFORMATION

"400" Trail Headquarters
Toll Free (800) 844-3507
Phone (608) 524-2850
Email reedsbrg@mwt.net
Web www.400statetrail.org

Elroy Commons
Toll Free (888) 606-2453
Phone (608) 462-2410
Email elroywi@mwt.net
Web www.elroywi.com

Hillsboro State Trail
Phone (608) 489-2521
Web www.hillsborowi.com

Reedsburg Chamber of Commerce
Toll Free (800) 844-3507
Email webmaster@reedsburg.org
Web www.reedsburg.org

LODGING

Motels/Resorts

Reedsburg

Comfort Inn
2115 E. Main St
Phone (608) 524-8535
Fax (608) 524-6570

Copper Springs Motel
E7278 Hwy 23/33
Phone (608) 524-4312
Fax (608) 524-9767
Email chanson@jvlnet.com
Web www.copperspringsmotel.com

Motel Reedsburg
1133 E. Main St
Toll Free (800) 526-6835
Phone (608) 524-2306

Super 8
1470 E. Main St.
Toll Free (800) 800-8000
Phone (608) 524-2888

Voyageur Inn
200 Viking Dr. (Hwy H)
Toll Free (800) 444-4493
Phone (608) 524-6431

Union Center

Garden City Motel
Hwy 80-82-33
Phone (608) 462-8253

Bed and Breakfast

Hillsboro

Debello Guest House
Phone (608) 489-3728

Inn Serendipity Woods Cabin
Phone (608) 329-7056
Web www.innserendipity.com

LaValle

Demaskie Den Guest House
102 North East St
Phone (608) 985-7426

Mill House on Main
203 East Main St
Phone (608) 985-7900
Web www.millhouseonmain.com

Reedsburg

Lavina Inn
325 Third St
Phone (608) 524-6706

Parkview B&B
211 North Park Street
Phone (608) 524-4333

Camping

Hillsboro

Hillsboro City Park
Phone (608) 489-2521

Reedsburg

Lighthouse Rock Campground
S 2330 County Hwy V
Phone (608) 524-4203

Wonewoc

Baker's Field Park
Phone (608) 464-3114

Chapparal Campground
S320 Hwy 33
Phone (608) 464-3944

Wonewoc Legion Park
Pine Street
Phone (608) 464-3114

GROCERIES

Hillsboro

County Market
(608) 489-2423

Greg's Market
(608) 489-2326

GROCERIES cont'd

Reedsburg
Viking Village Food
(608) 524-6108

Village Market
(608) 524-4533

BIKE RENTAL

La Valle
Trail Break
Phone (608) 985-8464

Reedsburg
Chamber of Commerce
Toll Free (800) 844-3507
Email webmaster@reedsburg.org
Web www.reedsburg.org

BIKE REPAIR

Reedsburg
Baraboo River Bike Shop
Phone (608) 524-0798

FESTIVALS AND EVENTS

Hustler

August
Hustler Fest
Parade, tractor pull, 3 on 3 basketball, carnival rides, games, music and dancing, three day event. Fourth Weekend
Phone (608) 847-9389

Reedsburg

June
Butter Festival
Parade, carnival rides, tractor and truck pulls, arts and crafts, Butter Run, music and food, Nishan Park, Father's Day weekend
Toll Free (800) 844-3507
Phone (608) 524-2850
Web www.reedsburg.org

August
Little League Tournament
First Weekend
Toll Free (800) 844-3507
Phone (608) 524-2850
Web www.reedsburg.org

October
Harvest Fest
Downtown Main Street, arts and crafts, contests, music, auto displays, food, First Saturday
Toll Free (800) 844-3507
Phone (608) 524-2850
Web www.reedsburg.org

ALTERNATE ACTIVITIES

Camp Douglas
Mill Bluff State Park
Primitive camping, picnic shelters, swimming beach, hiking trails, beautiful rock formations. Open Memorial Day–Labor Day.
Phone (608) 427-6692
Web www.dnr.state.wi.us

Wisconsin National Guard Library and Museum
Located at historic Volk Field, museum is housed in an 1896 log lodge that has been restored to its original appearance, exhibits, dioramas, video and slide programs. Outdoors view aircraft, artillery and tanks on static display.
Phone (608) 427-1280
Web www.volkfield.ang.af.mil

LaValle
Carr Valley Cheese Company
100 years of family cheesemaking, fresh curds daily, self-guided tours, open Mon–Sat
Toll Free (800) 462-7258
Phone (608) 986-2781
Web www.carrvalleycheese.com

E-Z Roll Riding Stable
Guided trail rides Apr 1-Sept. 1 or call for reservations for weekend rides anytime
Phone (608) 985-7722

Reedsburg
Exhibit of Norman Rockwell Art
Large collection of Norman Rockwell Art. Located at the Voyager Inn.
Toll Free (800) 444-4493
Phone (608) 524-6431
Web www.voyageurinn.com

Park Lane Model Railroad Museum
3,000 models of trains, farm tractors, fire trucks and cars, operating layouts in 'N', 'Z' and 'HO' scales, open mid May-mid Sept.
Phone (608) 254-8050

Reedsburg Area Historical Society
Pioneer log village, 1890 log homes, church, blacksmith shop and school in settlement, weekend afternoons Memorial Day through Labor Day
Toll Free (800) 844-3507
Phone (608) 524-2850

Military Ridge Trail

Vital Information:

Trail Distance: 37 miles

Trail Surface: limestone

Access Points: Dodgeville, Ridgeway, Barneveld, Blue Mounds, Mount Horeb, Verona

Fees and Passes: Wisconsin State Trail Pass; $3 daily fee or $10 for an annual pass. State Trail passes are good on all Wisconsin State Trails.

Trail Website: www.dnr.state.wi.us

ABOUT THE TRAIL

Formerly a Chicago and North Western Railway, the trail follows the top of Military Ridge, the divide between the watersheds of the Wisconsin River, to the north, and the Pecatonica and Rock Rivers to the south. It comes off the ridge just east of Mount Horeb and drops nearly 400 feet into the Sugar River Valley. The drop is very gentle, 2% to 5%, and the changing terrain makes the eastern part of the trail quite interesting. Agriculture, woodlands, wetlands and prairies border the trail.

TRAIL HIGHLIGHTS

The Riley Tavern, in Riley, has been a watering hole for bicyclists for at least four decades. Stop in for a laid back slice of life. The most interesting part of the trail runs between Mount Horeb and the trailhead near Verona. The trail climbs slowly from east to west, often along the sides of hills, and passes through a mix of natural and agricultural landscapes. The trail runs near Highway 151/18 for most of the distance from Mount Horeb to Ridgeway where the noise and barrenness of the Highway take away much of the pleasure of riding. The scenery improves again halfway between Ridgeway and Dodgeville as the trail veers from the highway and offers some great scenic vistas to the north. Blue Mound State Park offers swimming and scenic overlooks. Governor Dodge State Park has a full range of recreation facilities. The 60 year old Depot in Ridgeway is undergoing a complete restoration.

ABOUT THE ROADS

This is the Driftless Area of Wisconsin, ideal for dairy farms, paved lightly traveled roads and big hills. The opportunities for exploring are endless. Try the routes on these maps. If you get hooked on the area, stop in Madison at one of the bike shops and ask for more route information. You'll learn about more miles of good roads than you can possibly ride.

ROAD HIGHLIGHTS

The loop near Dodgeville offers everything the trail misses: hills and valleys, scenic vistas, constantly changing terrain and quiet roads. The hills are long; occasionally a mile or more of climbing. For a short, flat, out and back on a quiet road, take the Klevinville-Riley Road to County Road P. It nestles in among wetland trees and small creeks. The southern loop starts low along the Sugar River Valley, then climbs and rolls mightily as it loops back to the trail.

HOW TO GET THERE

Verona is southwest of Madison on U.S. Highway 151/18. Take the County Road PB exit and turn right at the end of the ramp. You will be on the west side of the highway and going north on Nesbitt Road. There isn't a sign for Nesbitt, so make sure you are NOT going south on PB towards Paoli. The trailhead is 1.1 miles north. All trail towns can be readily accessed via Highway 151/18. Trail access in Dodgeville is at the intersection of County Road YZ and Johns Street. Take County Rd YZ 0.2 miles east of Highway 23. See trail map.

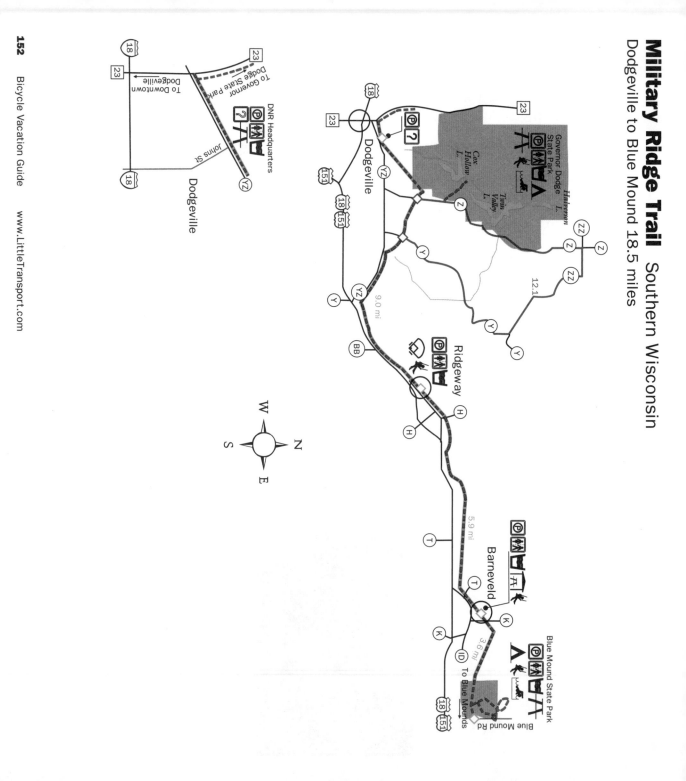

Military Ridge Trail

Southern Wisconsin
Dodgeville to Blue Mound 18.5 miles

Governor Dodge State Park

Halverson

Cox Hollow L.

Twin Valley L.

Dodgeville

9.0 mi

12.1

Ridgeway

5.9 mi

Barneveld

3.6 mi

Blue Mound State Park

Blue Mound Rd

To Blue Mounds

N
W · E
S

DNR Headquarters

To Governor Dodge State Park

To Downtown Dodgeville

Johns St

Dodgeville

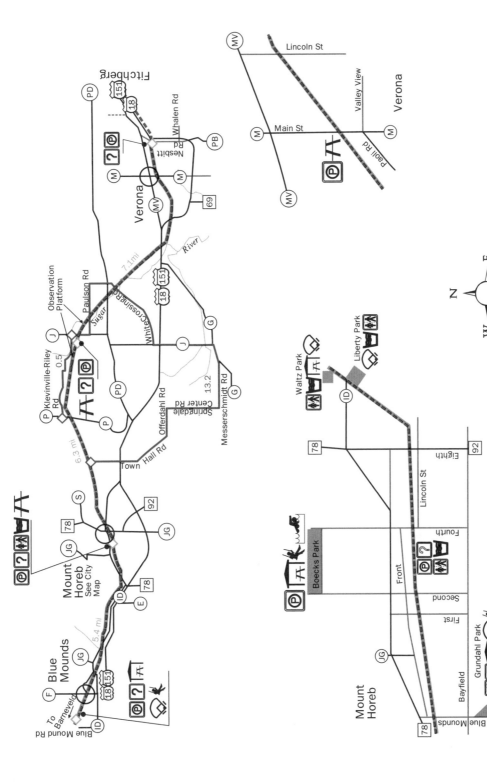

Lincoln St

MV

Valley View

Verona

M — Main St

M

Paoli Rd

MV

69

River

18 151

G

J

Messerschmidt Rd

G

Springdale

Center Rd

Offerdahl Rd

Whitecrossing Rd

18 151

Sugar

Paulson Rd

7.1 mi

13.2

Observation
Platform

J

0.5

P Klevinville-Riley Rd

PD

P

Town Hall Rd

6.3 mi

Fitchberg

PD

151

18

Whalen Rd

Nesbitt Rd

PB

M

Verona

MV

M

S

78

JG

92

JG

Mount Horeb
See City
Map

78

E

ID

5.4 mi

Blue Mounds

JG

F

18 151

ID

To Barneveld

Blue Mound Rd

Mount Horeb

Waltz Park

Liberty Park

ID

78

92

Eighth

Lincoln St

Fourth

Front

Boecks Park

Second

First

Grundahl Park

JG

Bayfield

Blue Mounds

78

N
W   E
S

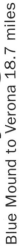

Military Ridge Trail

Southern Wisconsin

Dodgeville Chamber of Commerce
Toll Free (877) 863-6343
Phone (608) 935-5993
Fax (608) 930-5324
Email info@dodgeville.com
Web www.dodgeville.com

Military Ridge State Trail
Phone (608) 437-7393

Mount Horeb Area Chamber of Commerce
Toll Free (888) 765-5929
Phone (608) 437-5914
Email info@trollway.com
Web www.trollway.com

Verona Chamber of Commerce
Phone (608) 845-5777
Fax (608) 845-2519
Email info@VeronaWI.com
Web www.veronawi.com

Motels/Resorts

Dodgeville
Super 8 Motel
1308 Johns Street
Toll Free (800) 800-8000
Phone (608) 935-3888

Mount Horeb
Village Inn Motel

701 Springdale Street
Phone (608) 437-3350
Email edmoen@mhtc.net
Web www.littlebedder.com

Bed and Breakfast

Dodgeville
Grand View B & B
4717 Miess Road
Phone (608) 935-3261

Mount Horeb
Arbor Rose B&B
200 N. Second St
Phone (608) 437-1108
Email ArborRoseBandB@aol.com
Web arborrosebandb.com

Gonstead Guest Cottage
602 S. Second St
Phone (608) 437-4374
Email wall@mhtc.net
Web www.mthoreb.com/gonstead

Othala Valley Inn
3192 JG North
Phone (608) 437-2141
Email sleep@othalavalley.com
Web www.othalavalley.com

Verona
Beat Road Farm B&B
2401 Beat Rd
Phone (608) 437-6500
Email jrgira@aol.com
Web www.abarealty.com

Camping

Blue Mounds
Blue Mound State Park
Blue Mound Rd
Phone (608) 437-5711

Dodgeville
Governor Dodge State Park
4175 State Road 23 N
Phone (608) 935-2315

Blue Mounds
Blue Mounds Grocery
(608) 437-8027

Dodgeville
Dick's Supermarket
(608) 935-2366

Mount Horeb
Kalscheur's Fine Foods
(608) 437-3081

Trillium Natural Foods
(608) 437-5288

Verona
Miller & Son Supermarket
(608) 845-6478

Verona
Atkins Verona Bicycle Shoppe
Phone (608) 845-6644

Dodgeville
July
Dodgeville Blues Festival
A day of great Blues and Zydeco music.
Phone (608) 935-5993
Web www.dodgevillebluesfest.com

FESTIVALS AND EVENTS cont'd

Wisconsin Kiter Kite Making & Flying Workshop
Two days of kite flying & kite making workshops. The skies are alive with color and shapes.
Toll Free (877) 863-6343
Phone (608) 935-5993
Web www.dodgeville.com

Mount Horeb

June

Horribly Hill Hundred
A long, challenging, and very hilly bike ride. The worst, or best, in the Midwest. Check website for dates.
Toll Free (888) 765-5929
Phone (608) 437-5914
Web www.trollway.com

July

Art Fair
Held in conjunction with Sons of Norway Kaffe Stue, 110 artists on "Trollway" plus food, entertainment. Third Weekend
Toll Free (888) 765-5929
Phone (608) 437-5914
Web www.trollway.com

August

National Mustard Day
Mustard Games, Mustard tasting, visiting celebrities, refreshments. First Weekend
Toll Free (888) 765-5929
Phone (608) 437-5914
Web www.trollway.com

Verona

May

City Wide Garage Sale
Mother's Day Weekend
Phone (608) 845-5777
Web www.veronawi.com

Hometown Days Festival
Midway, family entertainment, concessions, bands, bicycle race, parade at Community Park. Check website for dates.
Phone (608) 845-5777
Web www.veronawi.com

ALTERNATE ACTIVITIES

Blue Mounds

Blue Mound State Park
Camping, observation towers, swimming pool and nature trails
Phone (608) 437-5711
Fax (608) 437-6214
Web www.dnr.state.us

Cave of the Mounds
Limestone cavern, rooms and galleries containing mineral deposits
Discovered in 1939, a registered National Natural Landmark
Phone (608) 437-3038
Fax (608) 437-4181
Email info@caveofthemounds.com
Web www.caveofthemounds.com

Little Norway
1856 Norwegian Farmstead and 'Stavkirke,' largest privately-owned collection of Norwegian antiques in the country
Phone (608) 437-8211
Email scwinner@earthlink.net
Web www.littlenorway.com

Dodgeville

Dolby Stables
One & two hour guided rides in Governor Dodge State Park, 45 minute ride on ranch, reservations helpful
Open May 1 to Nov 1.
Phone (608) 935-5205

Governor Dodge State Park
Wisconsin's second largest park, swimming, camping, boating, hiking
Phone (608) 935-2315
Web www.dnr.state.wi.us

Museum of Minerals and Crystals
Displays of rocks, minerals, crystals, and flourescents from around the world
Toll Free (877) 863-6343
Phone (608) 935-5205
Email info@dodgeville.com
Web www.dodgeville.com

Mount Horeb

Mt Horeb Pub and Brewery
Microbrewery located in historic creamery, hand crafted beers, tours available.
Phone (608) 437-4200

Mustard Museum
The world's largest collection of mustard, more than 3100 varieties
Toll Free (800) 438-6878
Phone (608) 437-3986
Email curator@mustardmuseum.com
Web www.mustardmuseum.com

Legend

▪▪▪▪▪ State or Regional Bike Trail

▪ ▪ ▪ City Bike Trail

▬▬▬ Bike Route on Road

Major Highway

Paved Road

Town Road
(gravel or unknown surface)

◇▬▬▬◇ 11.5 mi Mileage Between markers *
(State of Regional Trails only)

◇——◇ 6.4 Mileage Between Markers *
(Road Routes)

*Cyclometer readings will differ depending on tire pressure, riding style and computer settings. Your mileage may differ slightly from the stated distances.

🛈 Information Kiosk

Ⓟ Parking

🚻 Rest Rooms

🚰 Drinking Water

🛖 Sheltered Picnic Area

🌲 Picnic Bench

👫 Children's Play Area

🏊 Swimming Beach or Pool

⛺ Camping

 Hiking Trails

⛪ Church

⛳ Golf Course

🏛 Museum

✝ Cemetery

⚾ Baseball Field

🎿 Downhill Ski Area

🛶 Canoe Rental

🚤 Boat Launch

Revisions: Did you find a mistake? Did the trail change? We'd like to hear about it. Contact us at Little Transport Press, PO Box 8123, Minneapolis, MN 55408, or visit our website: www.LittleTransport.com

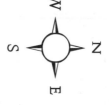